001.51
D6486

Volume IX, Number 8

Significant Issues Series

Gorbachev's Information Revolution

Controlling Glasnost in a New Electronic Era

Wilson P. Dizard and
S. Blake Swensrud

The Center for Strategic
and International Studies

Westview Press

**PUBLISHED IN COOPERATION WITH
THE CENTER FOR STRATEGIC AND INTERNATIONAL STUDIES,
WASHINGTON, D.C.**

The Center for Strategic and International Studies is a research organization founded in 1962 to foster scholarship and public awareness of emerging international issues on a broad, interdisciplinary basis. It is bipartisan and nonprofit. Its areas of research are selected in consultation with its governing bodies; and its work is entirely unclassified.

This Westview softcover edition is printed on acid-free paper and bound in softcovers that carry the highest rating of the National Association of State Textbook Administrators, in consultation with the Association of American Publishers and the Book Manufacturers' Institute.

Published in 1987 in the United States of America by Westview Press, Inc.; Frederick A. Praeger, Publisher; 5500 Central Avenue, Boulder, Colorado 80301

Library of Congress Cataloging-in-Publication Data
Dizard, Wilson P.
   Gorbachev's information revolution.
   (CSIS significant issues series, ISSN 0736-7136; v. 9, no. 8)
   1. Communication—Soviet Union.   2. Communication policy—Soviet Union.
3. Soviet Union—Politics and government—1982   .
I. Svensrud, S. Blake.   II. Title.   III. Series: Significant issues series;
v. 9, no. 8.   IV. Title: controlling glasnost in a new electronic era.
P92.S65D59   1987   001.51′0947   87-27914
ISBN 0-8133-7518-5

Composition for this book was provided by the authors.
This book was produced without formal editing by the publisher.

Printed and bound in the United States of America

∞ The paper used in this publication meets the requirements of the American National Standard for Permanence of Paper for Printed Library Materials Z39.48-1984.

6   5   4   3   2   1

Contents

About the Authors

Wilson P. Dizard is a senior fellow in international communications at the Center for Strategic and International Studies in Washington. He is also an adjunct professor of international affairs at the School of Foreign Service, Georgetown University. Before joining the Center, Mr. Dizard was a senior foreign service officer. His most recent publication is *The Coming Information Age* (New York: Longman Publishers, 2d ed., rev. 1985). Two additional publications by Dizard that touch on issues of this current study are *Television—A World View* (Syracuse, N.Y.: Syracuse University Press, 1966) and *The Strategy of Truth* (Washington: Public Affairs Press, 1961).

S. Blake Swensrud was a research assistant in the international communications program at the Center for Strategic and International Studies during the preparation of this study. A graduate of Tufts University, he is currently in the graduate international affairs program at George Washington University.

Foreword

The global information revolution, which has had a tremendous impact on all aspects of life in Western democracies, is beginning to affect the various communist countries, including the Soviet Union itself. That regime, rising from the ashes of an empire traditionally aloof from other societies, apprehensive of subversive movements, and secretive about its inner workings, has operated almost from the beginning on the principle of maintaining an information monopoly.

The Western lead in the new communications technologies makes possible a greater circulation of information from the West to Soviet-bloc populations, despite regime efforts to keep it out. At the same time, these technologies are becoming increasingly indispensable to the industrial and military strength and to the growth and smooth functioning of the economies of all developed countries, including the Soviet Union.

In the mass media and the cultural fields, the communist regime would prefer to keep out information or cultural influences from abroad, while the West is interested in seeing that such information gets in. In the science and technology fields, and particularly in computerization and advanced telecommunications, it is the Soviet Union and other communist countries that want to bring the latest information in, while the West (led by the United States), for national security reasons, would rather keep the most advanced of this information out of communist hands.

By comparison with developments in the West, the Soviets have been plagued by the relative failure of their scientific and technological sectors to come up with innovative discoveries and practical applications beneficial to the Soviet economy. This failure is attributable to the communication flow problems within the Soviet scientific and technical community—problems directly related to regime reluctance to give up its monopoly on information.

For decades, elements within the Soviet Union have understood the need to overcome the lack of scientific innovation and to introduce greater modernization and quality control in industry as well as the key role microelectronics (in computerization and telecommunications) must play in this process. Their efforts have been resisted by the traditionalists or conservatives who have equated openness to the West with vulnerability to ideological subversion.

It appears that Mikhail Gorbachev has made a calculated decison to side with the nontraditionalists. Wilson Dizard and S. Blake Swensrud have cogently analyzed Gorbachev's *perestroika* and its relationship to the information revolution. There are those who argue that for Gorbachev, the real goal is *perestroika*, while *glasnost* is only a means incidental to that goal. History and logic, however, lead to the conclusion that for the Soviets to respond adequately to the impelling force of the global information revolution, *glasnost* and *perestroika* are equally required.

Dr. Walter R. Roberts
Diplomat in Residence, The George Washington University
Former Associate Director, U.S. Information Agency

1

The Gorbachev Challenge

In the early years after the Russian revolution, Leon Trotsky reportedly proposed to Stalin that a modern telephone system be built in the new Soviet state. Stalin brushed off the idea, saying, "I can imagine no greater instrument of counter-revolution in our time."

This incident reflects the traditional ambivalence of Soviet leaders between the need for an adequate national communications system and the fear of losing control of their information monopoly. One result is that the USSR has the lowest per capita distribution of telephones among the industrialized nations—10 per 100 citizens. Most other civilian communications resources are equally poor.

In Mikhail Gorbachev's Soviet Union, pragmatic needs are forcing a new look at the dilemma between tight information control and economic efficiency. In his campaign to shake up the economy, the Soviet leader's biggest gamble may be his plans for a massive upgrading of communications and information facilities, from ordinary telephones to high-tech computers. Whether he succeeds will not be clear for a long time. What is clear is that Gorbachev is intent on moving toward a Soviet version of a Western information-based economy.

The outside world's attention in this area has been focused on one aspect of Gorbachev's information policies—the so-called *glasnost* campaign, aimed at providing more credible content in Soviet media and the arts. Glasnost (openness) has already had the effect of appearing to legitimize the new leader's agenda of economic and social reforms. It is a potentially hopeful factor in the prospect for a long-term evolution toward a more open, less repressive society. One of the hallmarks of such an evolution will be the modification, and eventual phasing out, of long-standing controls over communications and information resources.

The glasnost campaign is a small step in this direction. In its present form, its effects are largely limited to centralized media channels where the leadership can control its form and pace. More fundamental changes in the Soviet information environment will not happen until ordinary citizens gain greater access to networks of telephones, computers, and other electronic facilities in ways that will give them greater personal control over information. Viewed in this light, Gorbachev's plans for expanding these facilities have implications for the Soviet future well beyond his economic rationale for the project. This study will examine the Gorbachev initiatives in these sectors and their implications for Soviet society as well as for the world beyond Soviet borders.

The New Agenda

Although many of the details of the new telecommunications and computer projects are not known, the general outline has been broadly publicized in Soviet media. The Gorbachev agenda includes

- doubling the telephone system by the early 1990s,
- introducing computers and data bases at all levels of the national economy, and
- training a new generation, beginning with grade-school students, to become computer literate Soviet citizens.

Similar proposals have been a recurrent feature of Soviet economic plans for over two decades, with a wide gap between promises and results. Gorbachev clearly intends to narrow if not close the gap. His initiatives are an attempt to bring the USSR into the mainstream of a major global change. Advanced communications and information facilities are transforming the world economic environment with socially and politically compelling effects. As the world's third largest economy, the Soviet Union already has significant resources in these sectors, particularly in the military-industrial area. Nevertheless, Gorbachev and his planners are acutely aware of the country's overall deficiencies and the dangers of slipping even further behind the West economically and technologically.

Internationally, the new telecommunications and information initiatives can have a long-term effect on the strategic balance between the USSR and the members of the North Atlantic Treaty Organization. As in the past, the Soviet military will have first call on the new resources, both for its own uses and for the large industrial structure that directly supports it. Viewed from Moscow, the technological and economic changes taking place in China pose additional pressures for the Soviet role in the global high-tech competition.

In the civilian sector, improved communications and information facilities can reduce the inefficiencies that have nagged the Soviet economy for decades. Further down the road, a reasonably efficient economy could make the Soviet Union a more significant player in the global economy. For the present, the country is in the anomolous position of being a major industrial power whose external trade involves primarily raw materials and energy resources. It operates, as Soviet specialist Thane Gustafson notes, outside the global technological cycle.

Another Soviet affairs expert, Frederick Starr, points out that "computers have emerged as the last best hope for making the old economy work."[1] They are essential to the success of the sweeping plans for restructuring the Soviet economy announced in June 1987. They also have a direct bearing on Mikhail Gorbachev's prospects for retaining his leadership role by delivering on the expansive goals he has set for the economy in the coming years.

Given these imperatives, the Gorbachev initiatives must be taken seriously, not merely as another round of party promises to be expunged or conveniently forgotten in the future. A major upgrading of Soviet communications and information resources— key components of his high-tech modernization drive—will take place in the coming decade. By the mid-1990s, the USSR should have advanced facilities in these sectors roughly comparable to current resources in the West.

A significant start has already been made. It is most apparent in the telecommunications field, where decisions on large-scale expansion of these resources were taken before Gorbachev officially came to power in 1985. A recent survey by the Telecommunications Industry Research Center in Britain projects 1987 telecommunications equipment expenditures in the USSR at the equivalent of $9.8 billion, an increase of 17 percent over the previous year. Among industrialized countries, this represents less than half of projected U.S. spending ($24.3 billion), but considerably more than the projections for either Japan ($7.1 billion) or Germany ($6.1 billion).[2] Even allowing for statistical hyperbole in figures based on Soviet data, it is clear that a major effort to upgrade the country's telecommunications plant is under way.

Comparable expenditure figures for Soviet computers and related equipment are more difficult to obtain. The USSR is a major producer of such equipment, with particular emphasis on larger machines. It has been slow to adapt to the new range of desktop computers that are common in the West. Nevertheless, Soviet planners are shifting their priorities toward the smaller machines.

Even if the planned expansion of communications resources is only moderately successful, it can have an important effect in improving both the economy and the day-to-day living standards in the USSR. In a society where citizens are resigned to accepting small benefits from large promises, such incremental improvements can strengthen Gorbachev's credibility. Moreover, there is the glasnost factor—the potentially destabilizing effects of the new facilities on the Soviet leadership's ability to maintain its present level of information control.

The prospect of the Soviet leadership losing its present level of control over information is strongly influenced by the current younger generation being the most highly educated in the country's history. Among other attributes, this generation is better prepared by training and inclination to manage the vast amounts of information needed by an advanced industrial society. If previous practice is followed, there will be stringent controls on the new facilities to assure that they are focused primarily on the leadership's priorities. Nevertheless the proposed changes involve more than the addition of another set of resources like automobiles or housing. The Soviets will learn what the West has already found out, namely, that rapid expansion of high-tech communications and information resources results in a wide range of unplanned and unintended social and political effects such as job dislocations and legal practices.

Western observers have made widely divergent predictions about the potential impact of these changes within the USSR. These predictions range from a high-tech reversion to Stalinist controls to the overthrow of the present regime by a newly enlightened citizenry. The more probable scenario lies among these extremes, involving an evolution toward liberalized controls rather than violent change. The eventual outcome will be determined in part by power struggles between old-line officials and the new technocratic elite. If expanded information resources are to be efficiently exploited in the USSR, the current balance of power between technocrats and party members will have to be redefined, with critical political and social impact. The current leadership will have to co-opt the growing body of technocrats who have the expertise to manage the new high-tech facilities. This, in turn, will add a new level of complexity to the West's relations with the USSR. Beyond the need to contain Soviet military capabilities, there is little agreement in the West on how to deal with the changes within the Soviet Union that will come with the expanded communications and information resources (among other developments).

The complexities can be summarized, simplistically but usefully, in a shorthand phrase used over the years by Soviet-watchers: the "fat Russian/thin Russian" debate. The fat-Russian scenario identifies the long-term interest of the West with trying to influence Soviet behavior through liberalized trade and other steps that might encourage the country's development as a more prosperous, and presumably more peaceful, society. The thin-Russian scenario sees the West's best interest as aspiring to manage the decline of the present Soviet structure to a point where a less militaristic, more humane and democratic society can evolve.

The real-life options are, of course, considerably more complicated than choosing between hypothetical fat and thin Russians. The United States and other Western countries have relatively limited abilities to affect Soviet political and social patterns. Decisions about influencing the pattern of communications and information resources are particularly complex. The increasing availability of these resources within the Soviet Union adds a new dimension to Western strategy. It is a question not only of fatter Russians but also of better informed Russians.

Postindustrial Goals

The Gorbachev high-tech initiatives have a purpose beyond the accretion of more and better industrial resources. It involves the perception by the leadership of the evolution of the USSR as a postindustrial state. The new Soviet leadership is intent on demonstrating that only under its version of socialism can the new technologies be properly exploited. Mikhail Gorbachev's plans reach back to the Leninist formulation of "revolutionary fervor and American efficiency" as a guide for the alternate postindustrial society.[3] His focus is on economic reform, and it is not misplaced. With two decades of steadily declining growth rates, the Soviet economy is losing momentum at a time when the United States and other advanced countries are preparing for the technologies of the twenty-first century.

The Gorbachev high-tech initiatives, if successful, will permit the current leadership to begin to redeem promises made over the past seven decades about the party's ability to make the Soviet economy work more efficiently. In the early 1960s, Nikita Khrushchev told Soviet citizens that they would have the highest standard of living in the world by 1980. Mikhail Gorbachev is more realistic in his blueprint for the Soviet future. The 1986 economic program adopted by the Twenty-seventh Party Congress promises to double output by the end of the century with special attention to consumer goods and services. Based on previous performance, it is likely there will be slippages in meeting this goal. It would be a mistake, however, to underestimate either the intentions or the capabilities of the Soviets. The USSR already has a respectable computer-based production and planning infrastructure. Moreover, the Soviet government has a proved ability to marshal resources for purposes it considers important, even if the effort involves considerable waste and other inefficiencies.

There is a critical difference between Soviet and Western approaches to mass computerization and communications. The

West is going through a rapid, disorganized, technology-driven expansion period characterized by shifts in political and economic power. In expanding Soviet information resources, Gorbachev is not catching up as much as adapting a limited part of Western expertise and experience to autarchic political and economic needs.

For the Soviet communications and computer initiatives, the emphasis is on managed change with particular attention to maintaining control over communications and information, which are at the heart of the ruling party's claim to power. Previous Soviet leaders have maintained tight control over limited resources. The Gorbachev approach is riskier. In expanding telecommunications and information facilities, he has to consider the erosion of long-standing controls. As Soviet computer specialist and Academy of Sciences member Andrei P. Ershov has acknowledged, "Computerization will cause changes. A society has to adapt to new technologies, even if that means changing the legal structure of that society."[4]

The overall purpose of the new initiative is to serve government military and industrial needs—an electronic expansion of present priorities. In a sense, it is replicating what initially happened in the West in the 1960-1980 period when advanced communications and information resources were applied primarily to large-scale industrial and military uses. The Gorbachev initiatives are an attempt to close the gaps left by his predecessors who neglected to keep pace with the West in these sectors. Another purpose is to improve the general standard of Soviet life by a more equal redistribution of capital resources between consumer goods and heavy industrial production. Gorbachev is faced with the difficult task of shifting the Soviet economy away from the labor-intensive Stalinist model to a more high-tech, service-oriented model.

During Gorbachev's first two years in office, his high-tech plans were marked by considerable rhetoric and goal-setting. The June 1987 decision on restructuring key parts of the economy was a bold step toward basic reform. Nevertheless, the implementation of these changes has, initially at least, been cautious. In part this can be attributed to internal Kremlin debates, which have marked

Gorbachev's consolidation of power in these early years. The somber warnings of his more realistic economic advisers often take second place to the political maneuvering between party, military, and other power centers.

For the present, it is significant that Gorbachev recognizes the need to take decisive steps toward an advanced postindustrial environment. In some ways, his approach is comparable to the industrialization drive of the Stalin period. There is, however, an essential difference between the Stalin era's industrialization experience and the current situation. Traditional industrial facilities could more easily be centrally managed and controlled than is possible today. Even in the face of considerable waste and loss of efficiency, forced industrialization transformed the Soviet economy. In the Stalin era, the focus was on quantitative production; Gorbachev faces the more difficult problem of qualitative production—a task that calls for heavy reliance on high-tech facilities.

The large-scale applications of communications and of information resources in particular present strikingly different problems. For over 60 years, limited Soviet resources in these sectors have been contained within the party's control mechanisms. Copying machines and telephones were available almost exclusively to politically reliable enterprises and individuals. Similiar controls were placed on the computers that were installed in workplaces in the late 1950s and 1960s. The large mainframe machines typical of that period were located in centralized facilities where their use could be monitored.

This mainframe experience still influences the thinking of many Soviet officials regarding computerization. Centrally controlled mainframes have served the state reasonably well up to now. If more advanced use of computers is to be encouraged, however, the USSR will have to adapt to the dynamic shifts occurring in the technology. As the West is demonstrating, mainframes will continue to be important, but the focus is now on the large-scale dispersion of smaller computer facilities and networks.

For the Soviet Union, a similar shift would necessitate a wider dispersal of communications and information resources than has ever been considered in its history. A new balance will need to be struck between centralized direction and opening up information resources to an increasingly educated population.

The West is now going through the creative destruction that economist Joseph Schumpeter saw as the characteristic of periods of major technological change. The shifts are often traumatic as older industries wither, newer ones come to the fore, and ordinary people's lives, as well as the best-laid plans of the experts, are disrupted. At the same time, there is a general acceptance of the need for changes in social patterns and political power in ways that reinforce democratic values as well as economic growth.

A somewhat parallel debate is taking place in the USSR within a different ideological context. Old-line Marxist-Leninist doctrine on the "scientific-technological revolution" (STR) has been dusted off to accommodate the new realities of microelectronics. In a typical explication, two Soviet Academy of Sciences members declared in a 1984 *Voprosy Filosofii* (*Philosophical Questions*) article:

> Thus we see that the development of microelectronics has logically led to a new stage in the scientific and technological revolution at a time when human civilization has entered an age of robots and information science that transform the production sphere and the entire life of modern man. . . . Socialist society fully evaluates the revolutionary potential and social consequences of microelectronics, information science, and biotechnology. It opens up broad opportunities for such applications and, at the same time, in its very essence corresponds most fully to this new technology, which requires that vast social capital rather than private capital—even if it may exceed the material resources of socialism for a period of time— be brought into play (on a planned basis). The socialist social structure makes it possible to use the basic potential of the new technology—its labor-saving character—to the fullest.[5]

(Additional excerpts from the *Voprosy Filosofii* article can be found in appendix 4.)

Ideology aside, many Soviet planners understood the implications of computerization before Mikhail Gorbachev added his authority to the subject. The imperative to computerize was emphasized by Anatoliy Aleksandrov, then president of the Soviet Academy of Sciences, in a January 1984 *Izvestia* article. The development of the next generation of computers, he said, was of paramount importance, comparable to the space or missile races. Despite technological embargoes by the United States, he continued, "We have overcome problems of no less complexity, such as the creation of an atomic bomb and space rocket technology. Our science and technology was able to develop these by itself, and in a short time as well."[6]

Despite these brave words, the transition to a more information-intensive, service-based economy will be difficult. As one example, unemployment—long a taboo subject in the USSR— is now being publicly discussed as the first guarded steps are taken to plan how to deal with labor dislocations, which are the result of restructuring aimed at improving efficiency. Retraining and relocating millions of ordinary workers will be difficult at best. One Soviet economist has suggested that as many as 19 million factory workers will have to be reassigned to the services sector as a result of labor-saving technologies and management practices.[7] More significant may be the subtle effects that a more service-oriented economy will have on political and social patterns.

Computers and Economic Reform

A critical factor in determining Soviet postindustrial patterns will be the leadership's ability to implement its June 1987 decisions modifying long-standing command-economy practices. The party's Central Committee, clearly dominated for the first time by Gorbachev, ordered extensive changes in Soviet economic management. These changes included an end to fixed, subsidized prices and the loosening of centralized controls over thousands of state enterprises. The committee called for a "drastic expansion" in the independence of enterprises and "an emphatic reduction of central interference in the day-to-day operations of subordinate economic units." At the time, Soviet officials estimated that only 25 to 30 percent of manufacturing would be conducted under government control by the early 1990s.[8]

The success of these reforms will depend heavily on continued large-scale expansion of telecommunications and information resources. Not only will more facilities be needed than are currently planned, but they will have to be configured in new ways to meet the needs of an economy where, by government fiat, decision making and related production and distribution activities will become more dispersed. The new reforms call for a greatly diminished role for Gosplan, the state planning committee, which has long controlled the economy in such areas as the flow of raw materials to plants and the setting of prices. The June 1987 restructuring of the economy (*perestroika*) envisages the development of direct links between manufacturing plants and the suppliers of raw materials, with wholesale prices set by contract between the organizations. This implies the expansion of telecommunications and computer links that are now weak or nonexistent. Conversely, it suggests considerably less reliance on large centralized mainframe machines (such as those operated by Gosplan) in favor of small computers and data bases. The result could be to upgrade dramatically the use of dispersed data networks throughout the USSR, a development with political as well as economic implications.

Despite the proposed reforms, the key question remains: Can computers and other high-tech resources be fit effectively into an economic format that still contains large elements of centralized controls? There can be no doubt about the Gorbachev commitment to advanced technology. It is a theme that can be traced back to his early months in power, beginning with an April 1985 speech before the party Central Committee, barely a month after he took office. Gorbachev laced his high-tech vision with sharp criticism of officials who were allegedly blocking progress in this area. He returned to this criticism in his Central Committee speech in June 1987 outlining the new economic reforms. After describing the country's other economic weaknesses, he noted:

The most alarming thing, perhaps, is that we began to lag behind in scientific and technical development. At a time when countries in the West had begun on a broad scale the restructuring of the economy with emphasis on resource saving, the use of the latest technologies, and other achievements of science and technology, our scientific and technical progress was retarded. This was not because of the absence of scientific groundwork but chiefly for the reason that the national economy was not receptive to innovations.[9]

In stressing the lack of receptivity to innovation, Gorbachev was returning to one of his earlier themes—the need for improved management procedures. Soon after taking office in 1985, he expanded the range of mildly decentralized management experiments begun by his predecessor and mentor, Yuri Andropov. He also created a system of incentives to reward productivity gains. The changes included cuts in bonuses and fines for managers who do not shape up. These pressures may provoke a new respect for the advantages of computers and other high-tech resources among previously reluctant Soviet managers, now faced with the need to implement the decentralization reform plans announced in June 1987.

Such a shift will have to reverse a long history of difficulties in integrating computers into the Soviet economic system.[10] The primary rationale for using computers in the Soviet economy, as in any other, is to promote more efficient use of resources, with particular attention to planning and identifying changing requirements in the system. This rationale assumes an environment that accepts the need for changes and rewards the managers who make them. But the environment has been weak; there has been a systemic bias in the Soviet economy favoring conservative choices. In part, this bias results from the lack of effective incentive systems in which the rewards are commensurate with the risks involved.

For the present, bureaucratic opposition and inertia are still formidable factors in slowing economic change. As Soviet economics specialist Marshall Goldman notes:

> The Soviet bureaucracy is perhaps the greatest obstacle to reform because such reform threatens their hold on power and their economic well-being. Short of some radical purge or institutional upheaval, the likelihood is that Party and bureaucratic interference will continue as before.[11]

The available evidence suggests that while Gorbachev is moving energetically down the path to reform, he has not achieved a revolutionary purge or institutional upheaval. Although he has eliminated a number of obstacles in a remarkably short time, the extent to which he will be able to institutionalize these changes and keep the system dynamic remains in question. Latent innovative forces within the Soviet economy will still be hobbled by a system in which power is heavily concentrated at the echelons that resist surrendering decision-making authority. Party leaders may find themselves increasingly torn between unpleasant computer-generated options that challenge their own ideological instincts and training. Whatever the imperatives of economic efficiency, it will be difficult for senior Soviet bureaucrats to give up a significant amount of their party-knows-best power to inanimate machines or to the technocrats who program them.

Military considerations are another critical factor in the new drive to upgrade communications and information capabilities. The starting point is that key elements of Soviet industry are divided into civilian and military sectors. The two sectors have essentially operated in the past on parallel tracks with relatively little crossover. The separation is particularly pronounced in sensitive high-tech areas like telecommunications and computers where military needs usually have the first call on research and development resources.

In his recent pronouncements on the Soviet economy, Gorbachev has indicated the need for closer cooperation between the military and civilian industrial sectors, particularly in transferring military research results. He is said to be impressed by the degree to which technological spin-offs from the West's military research and development (R&D) programs have been incorporated in civilian industries. Such a change will probably not happen quickly as it involves a major departure from Soviet industrial practices. The process may, in fact, be made more difficult as the military focuses on developing responses to the ultra-tech U.S. Strategic Defense Initiative (SDI). In any case, increased computer use in the military provides an important training ground for a new generation of computer-wise Soviet citizens.

The Yuppie Factor

The chief beneficiaries of the new resources in the civilian sector
are the large and growing group of young urban professionals, the
Soviet version of Western Yuppies. As much as these Soviet
careerists may privately grumble about the system, they can be
counted on, at least initially, to go along with government controls
over the new facilities. For the most part, Soviet professionals
have accepted restrictions in communications and other areas in
exchange for limited but real improvements in living standards
and career prospects. They already have greater access to more
"outside" information than any previous Soviet generation
through job-related contacts as well as through such channels as
shortwave radio, Western videotapes, and privileges at specialized
libraries and data centers.

In the coming decade, even greater access to non-Soviet
information resources will be possible as more telecommunications and computer-terminal facilities linked to foreign and
domestic data banks become available. The major shift among
younger professionals will be attitudinal; they will begin to regard
greater information access more as a prerogative than a privilege.
Although this shift is not fertile ground for organized dissidence, it
suggests a changed environment in which toleration of information restrictions begins to narrow as familiarity with the new
resources increases.

The talents and commitment of these professionals are a vital
resource in the Gorbachev high-tech initiatives. It is, of course,
difficult to characterize the attitudes and feelings of such a varied
and amorphous group. The stake of these professionals in the system, however, seems to be defined more by personal and professional rewards in their careers than by commitment to the party
bureaucracy, official ideology, or even the traditional appeals to
Russian patriotism—attitudes that make them suspect in the eyes
of more orthodox party leaders. This factor can affect professional
access to computers and data bases. As Ivan Selin of American
Management Systems notes, "Since information is a high prestige
field, the Party is loathe to allow real control to the scientific community; within this community, access to choice assignments

[involving computers] goes to senior people as rewards rather than the junior people who could contribute the most."[12] The increasing need to rely on this group of young technocrats will require modifications in this policy.

There is evidence that the new leadership is acutely aware of changing attitudes among young professionals. Soviet society has moved well beyond the old workers-and-peasants pattern; it is increasingly urbanized and better educated. The first truly post-war generation is now mature. The members of this generation are generally less likely to accept conditions of economic deprivation than were their parents who lived through forced industrialization and the war years. In May 1985, Gorbachev referred to the new breed of citizen as "a person with broad cultural and political horizons and sophisticated intellectual needs" who would not listen to oversimplified answers and worn-out clichés. This description was an indirect acknowledgement of a generational shift in which there will be greater resistance, largely passive, to vague party promises and simplistic solutions about "the further perfection" of Soviet society. The growth in numbers and importance of Soviet-style Yuppies is creating a rising tide of expectations for greater quality and quantity of consumer goods, information, and other privileges.

The role of information resources in achieving such improvements will depend heavily on two factors—permitting broad distribution of small computers and upgrading the quality of the information handled by these machines. There will probably be significant progress in both these areas within the next four to five years, given the pressure to show results. One outcome, over a period of time, will be marginal losses in central control over the new facilities and the information flowing through them.

The willingness to acknowledge, in the glasnost campaign, failures in the party's traditional approach to information is significant in itself. Now the question is what further steps the new Gorbachev leadership will take to adapt long-standing information controls to the realities of a more sophisticated, better educated citizenry. The answer will set the tone and direction for the Soviet version of a postindustrial information-intensive society.

In a relatively short time, the glasnost campaign has had a distinct impact on the media's handling of information about faults and failings in Soviet society. The practice is not new; newspapers have often performed a safety-valve function in the past by "exposing" small-scale scandals and other improprieties. Gorbachev has stepped up this practice and expanded it to the more important medium of television. For the first time, viewers are being treated to a Soviet version of investigative reporting into alleged misdeeds, complete with call-in shows where government officials respond to citizen questions. National disasters such as the Chernobyl nuclear accident, the sinking of a cruise ship in the Black Sea, and political riots in the Ukraine have received print and broadcast coverage, a clear departure from the traditional norm. At another level, Mikhail Gorbachev himself has become a familiar TV figure, appearing in carefully staged street encounters with ordinary citizens.

Some Western analysts interpret the glasnost intiative as a sign of liberalization. They suggest that it represents a sign of greater reliance on public opinion, citing as an example the Gorbachev proposal of multiple candidacy and secret balloting in elections. The hard evidence for any significant liberalization remains slim, however.

The glasnost campaign has other motives. The first is to provide a controlled signal that the new leader acknowledges long-standing deficiencies in Soviet society and plans to do something about them. Another purpose is to put pressure on Soviet managers and regional administrators, particularly in the economic sector, to improve their performance by threatening to publicly expose their errors. In effect, these threats amount to controlled experiments of public accountability. Finally, through a show of Soviet objectivity, the glasnost program is designed to undercut the credibility of the increasingly available non-Soviet news and other information, most notably from Western radio broadcasts.

The result has been a degree of openness that is unusual— and in some cases unprecedented—in modern Soviet experience. The glasnost initiative is still, however, too ambiguous and limited to be measured for its longer-term impact on the Soviet information environment. The campaign itself has been spotty, in part because of cautious attitudes of party officials assigned to implement it. The new leadership has had problems convincing party media managers, particularly in provincial areas, to take up the campaign vigorously. Their reluctance is understandable: many of them are aware of previous glasnost-style projects that were suddenly ended, leaving the more enthusiastic practitioners exposed to party retribution. Furthermore, regional managers, journalists, and party leaders stand to lose if public accountability is established in their provinces.

There have been some additional spin-offs from the campaign. The most notable has involved pressure from Soviet writers and other artists for a lessening of censorship constraints on their work. Such complaints surfaced dramatically at the 1986 Writers Union Congress as many delegates tested the limits of the new policy. "The nation wants glasnost," poet Andrei Voznesensky declared at the meeting. "It knows the monstrous strength of evil, lawlessness, corruption, bribe-taking, deception, and double-dealing."[13] His speech, and others equally critical, were reported in the official media. In addition, party officials acceded to pressure from Writers Union members to publish Boris Pasternak's novel, *Dr. Zhivago*, ending a 30-year ban. An earlier decision to abolish *Glavlit*, the literary censorship agency, was another small step toward more openness in Soviet cultural life.

Glasnost Extended

Despite its limitations, the glasnost campaign sets the stage for the extension of the openness principle beyond the mass media. This prospect has particular relevance to the expanded telecommunications and computer resources called for under the Gorbachev high-tech plan. The effectiveness of these resources is directly tied to the quality of the information they deal with.

The new facilities can, of course, make the compiling and accessing of data dramatically more efficient. Information technology comes into its own when it enhances human creativity in analyzing problems on the basis of objectively testable and, therefore, reliable data. These conditions imply that the relevant information is available to everyone affected by it and that it can be effectively challenged and modified when necessary. Western and Soviet abilities to utilize electronically manipulated data effectively are often in dramatic opposition, especially with regard to the availability of the information as well as its ability to be challenged and modified.

The key element is the validity of data. The temptation to misuse computers and their data knows no boundaries. Data are "cooked" in Minneapolis and Munich as well as in Moscow. The test is whether there are effective means for checking the data against the realities of the problem in question. Such checks are more likely to happen in a system where information flows both horizontally and vertically, providing a built-in set of checks and balances favoring more reliable data. The explosive growth of desktop computing power, operating both up and across organizational layers, has the effect of both reinforcing and complicating this prospect. Large Western enterprises have their share of these problems as managers fear the loss of control as the data are dispersed, which increases the possibility that they will not get adequate information from units down the line.

Soviet managers, with a similiar need for efficient information flow, have the added burden of political constraints. Data movement is essentially vertical, to a central or regional bureaucracy. A built-in bias against networking exists when it has the appearance, if not the reality, of bypassing central planning procedures. The decentralization reforms mandated in the June 1987 Central Committee decree should have the effect of modifying these long-standing practices in the coming years.

Meanwhile, the USSR's high-tech project faces barriers both in the types of computers used and in the quality of information handled. The two subjects are related, of course, and each will require changes that go against deep-rooted Soviet practices.

The problem begins with the party's claim that it alone can define "Socialist reality," a writ that extends literally to the most minute facts and opinions throughout the Soviet system. Soviet-affairs analyst Robert C. Tucker has pointed out that, from the time of the 1917 revolution, none of the monopolies enjoyed by the party would be as crucial as its monopoly of language. "The ultimate weapon of political control," he noted, "would be the dictionary." Given this context, data in computers are simply another type of information to be manipulated and controlled. This fact is a powerful reality in assessing the prospects for Soviet computer and telecommunications expansion, both at home and in links to the outside world.

Mikhail Gorbachev and his colleagues must make choices that have long-term social, political, and ideological implications. In the near term, their efforts are concentrated on the particular problem of improving economic efficiency. The role of communications and information resources is very much involved in the debate between centralization or dispersal of decision making. The need to show results in the new modernization drive may increase the pressure for more decentralization of decision making beyond the June 1987 reform program, with greater reliance on dispersed information flow, including computer data bases and networking. The result—in addition to the prospect of more efficient operations—will be a steady erosion in central controls over the dispersed facilities and over the information flowing through them.

Controlling the New Machines

There are increasing indications that Soviet authorities are aware of these electronic threats to their information controls. The subject is usually handled indirectly through the use of code words familiar to all Soviet citizens. The basic message is clear, however. The primary control will be limiting the number of people who have access to the new communications and information devices. Such control will not be difficult in government establishments, where most of the new equipment will be installed. Somewhat more difficult to deal with will be personal computers, although their distribution will be carefully monitored. A 1985 discussion of computerization by the journal *Nauka i Zhizn* (*Science and Life*) suggested that those benefiting from the computer expansion program will be "for the most part people who are already familiar with computer technology and have a good grasp of it."[14] The inference that computers will be placed only in trusted hands would not have been missed by Soviet readers.

The warnings are also spelled out in mass publications. In a 1985 *Pravda* article on the rapid expansion of computers, a leading computer expert, A.P. Ershov, warned of dangers that "should be a matter for careful observation and not be allowed to get out of control." This applies, he added, to the introduction of universal computer training: "The task of introducing electronic computers into the school and the approaches to its solution that are emerging is without precedent in history and must be carried out taking full account of our social system, its realities, and its cultural and social traditions." The code phrase about the realities of the social system should be enough to warn any *Pravda* reader naive enough to hope that a new age of computerized richness was at hand.[15] In a more specialized publication, *Soviet State and Law*, lawyer E.F. Melnik decries a tendency "in the matter of automatization to give priority to the technical aspects without taking into account the specific qualities of the existing system of organs of state administration." Again the code words bear a warning. Melnik underlines the point: "Automatization does not mean the appearance of new organs of control and certainly not a new system of managing the national economy. The system of organs of state administration has been functioning since the creation of Soviet power, improving and developing in accordance with the demands of social progress."[16]

The message is unmistakable: don't expect any big changes. Because the ordinary Soviet citizen has little immediate prospect of dealing with computers, it is a warning directed at the professionals who will be involved with new technologies. By and large, they are men and women who have learned politically to keep their heads down all their lives, beyond the standard activities necessary to advance their careers such as membership in a Communist youth organization. As a group, they are well aware of the consequences of being accused of an antisocial activity. Their attitude gives a hard edge to the Moscow joke about two men looking at a small computer displayed in a shop window:

Man 1: "How much do you think such a computer would cost me?"

Man 2: "Oh, I'd take a rough guess at two to five years in jail."

These cautious attitudes will restrain any impulses to shortcut official controls over expanded computer and communications facilities. A few well-publicized crackdowns will add conviction to warnings about misuse of the new resources.

The temptation to use these resources for other than officially approved purposes will also be tempered by the extensive electronic control mechanisms in the new facilities. Computer security techniques, in particular, have been vastly improved in recent years. American corporations spend tens of millions of dollars annually on sophisticated devices for controlling database access from local and remote terminals. Soviet authorities will do no less—and probably will do more—to limit access to their new facilities. Their initial efforts will be effective, but there will be some erosion in the process. Monitoring the telephone networks (and, by extension, the computers that can be plugged into them) will become increasingly difficult as the number of telephone instruments and small computers increases. Soviet authorities will be introduced for the first time to the computer hacker and his ability to break into allegedly secure systems.

Second, most of the data moving through the expanded facilities will be routine technical and administrative information, not the material of deep dissent or even mild protest. This detail notwithstanding, the new channels will be in place, and the prospect for using them for unauthorized purposes will be widened.

Nevertheless, the fact of greater access to these resources will have its own force. The shift will be a subtle one, stretched out over years. As computer facilities become more commonplace, the pressure from many professionals to ease restrictions will increase. For career, if not intellectual, reasons, educated Soviet citizens have the same natural inclination to expand their information horizon as do their Western counterparts. The more venturesome will seek to circumvent existing controls. In a reversal of the ways in which Western computer hackers break into networks, their Soviet counterparts will be more interested in breaking *out* of their controlled networks at home and, for the more daring, abroad.

In the current climate of political uncertainty, few Soviet professionals will be willing to risk hard-won career gains by unauthorized computer use. Any significant changes will take place only when and if there is a more discernible relaxation in the information environment within the USSR. The current expansion of telecommunications and computer resources could widen the prospects for such an evolution but cannot bring it about alone. Relaxation will require the convergence of other forces that erode the government's overall ability to maintain traditional controls. The new communications and computer facilities must be considered in the mix of influences on Soviet information patterns, such as the glasnost campaign, as well as the increasing availability of information from the West, in particular by shortwave radio.

Soviet authorities are aware of these prospects—present and potential—for erosion of information controls. They must balance this threat against the equally real prospect that the USSR will become a second-rate power economically if they continue to resist large-scale computerization.

How will Gorbachev and his advisers respond to these conflicting challenges? The answer, for the present, is not clear. Ideology will play an important role in their decisions. There is a mystique about computers in the USSR that surpasses any similar tendencies in the West. This is reflected in the vast cliché-clogged literature about the scientific-technological revolution and in particular its "new stage" since the introduction of computers.

Computers fit neatly into the Marxist-Leninist concept of a socialist society and its vision of a technology-powered workers' state. In his day, Lenin defined communism as Soviet power plus electrification. Today he would undoubtedly have added computers to the equation. His enthusiasm for an electronic utopia was later modified by Stalin who, to the point of paranoia, feared technologies that threatened to erode his control. The result was a massive setback in Soviet scientific progress, particularly in the post-World War II years when Western science was involved in an unusually creative period of research in communications and computer technology.

Official Soviet concern about ideology in this area seems irrelevant to most Westerners. It would be naive, however, to underestimate the role of ideology in the USSR. As Zbigniew Brzezinski notes:

Its importance lies in the influence of the ideological framework on more immediate, and otherwise quite well informed, policy judgments. Though far from committing Soviet leaders to short-term militancy, the ideological framework does inhibit them from thinking of accommodations and stability as ends in themselves, since that would be tantamount to negating the communist view of history as a fluid, dialectical process.[17]

These attitudes, as much as current economic realities, are driving Soviet high-tech modernization. Ideology aside, the men who run the USSR are pragmatists. The Gorbachev decision to expand computer and related resources involves unique risks and rewards. He and his colleagues are dealing with a power that could, in their own perception, bring about the triumph of communism. It is also a force that challenges their internal power base in unprecedented ways. Despite sophisticated control mechanisms, there will be a crossover point, somewhere in the future, when controls begin to erode and eventually to break down under the weight of the enormous amount of computer and communications resources needed by a modern industrial society.

Before examining the further implications of this prospect, it is useful to take a closer look at current developments in the Soviet communications and computer sectors and related areas.

2

The Telephone Connection

Mikhail Gorbachev's high-tech initiatives are heavily dependent on his ability to deal with a familiar technology—telephones and the networks that connect them. Such networks are the framework within which telephones, data banks, and other specialized services link computers to users. This process is well advanced in Western nations, where telecommunications facilities are being upgraded dramatically to handle the new services.

The Soviet Union lags in this area. With some important exceptions, its present telecommunications system is not designed to handle the expanded requirements of the new computerization drive. A good first-order measure of a country's ability to develop a high-tech economy is its per capita telephone ratio. The USSR has about 10 phones per 100 citizens. By comparison, the United States is approaching 100 percent distribution; most other industrialized nations have at least a 60 percent ratio.

This Achilles' heel has been acknowledged, implicitly at least, by the Gorbachev leadership in its plans to strengthen Soviet telecommunications, which will require an attitudinal shift with long-range political, economic, and social implications. Until now, adequate telecommunications facilities have been limited to key government and industrial sectors, including the military. Consumer communications—beginning with simple access to a telephone—has had low priority, despite official statements to the contrary. As in the past, the best of the new facilities will be allotted to government, industrial, and military sectors. There will, however, be an increase of personal access to telephones and related facilities. Urban professionals will be the initial beneficiaries of this change, but it will extend eventually to remote rural users. Although this increased access to telephones will be slow and uneven, its significance should not be underestimated. The eventual result will be a subtle change in the social environment, affecting the current pattern of communications and information controls throughout the USSR.

Expansion Plans

A February 1985 decision by the CPSU Central Committee and the USSR Council of Ministers marked a turning point in the modernization and expansion of the the Soviet telecommunications system.[18] Although Soviet media stressed the consumer benefits of the decision, the underlying purpose of the decision was to speed the development of a highly automated centralized telecommunication system for state purposes. (See appendix 1 for the full text of the Central Committee decision.) The need was originally addressed several years earlier in a less-publicized Central Committee decision intended to end the proliferation of the "private" (that is, dedicated or limited access) telecommunications networks that government organizations were developing to bypass the inefficiencies of the public system. Phasing out these alternate systems will give the central government more control over national telecommunications for security purposes.

The February 1985 Central Committee resolution was approved several weeks before Gorbachev took power. As a member of the committee, he was clearly in sympathy with the decision, a fact confirmed in his public statements and in policies laid down at the Twenty-seventh Party Congress in February 1986. The Central Committee's action in this case was an important step in plans to improve Soviet economic performance.

The exact nature of the new telecommunications initiative is still difficult to determine because information about communications facilities is generally treated as a state secret. The degree to which such information is restricted is illustrated in a long review of the accomplishments of the Eleventh Five-Year Plan in January 1986. The section on telecommunications developments consisted of one ambiguous sentence: "Communications enterprises met their output volume target and achieved an output rise of five percent."[19] Even the number of telephones in the USSR is a classified fact. Soviet statements on telephone density usually cite a figure of "around 30 million" instruments.

The telecommunications plan announced by the Central Committee in its 1985 decision is similarly short on details. Plan objectives are stated in vague percentages and ratios. There are, nevertheless, enough broad indicators to suggest the magnitude of the proposed upgrading. It calls for the construction of urban automatic telephone exchanges with a total capacity of 10 million lines during the current (1986-1990) Five-Year Plan. (No similar figure for rural exchanges is given.) This urban expansion would involve an increase of about one-third in overall telephone facilities in a very short time—a formidable goal that will undoubtedly slip. The resolution makes a special point of saying that "not less than 75 percent" of the new telephones provided for in the expansion will be assigned to "the population," a vague formulation suggesting that consumer needs are being considered.

Since the 1985 decision, commentaries by Soviet officials have somewhat expanded on these general statements. In a March 1985 radio address, M.A. Aleshin, a Ministry of Communications official, spoke of plans for tripling the number of telephones by the year 2000, giving the Soviet Union a telephone penetration of 90 million sets at that time—roughly one phone for every three persons.[20] By comparison, most other industrialized countries will have reached 100 percent penetration by the end of the century.

Aleshin and other Soviet commentators put heavy emphasis on expanding telephone service to Soviet homes. According to Aleshin, 23 percent of the families in urban areas and 7 percent living in rural areas had telephones in 1985. In addition to the acknowledged gap between urban and rural telephone distribution, wide differences in phone availability between Soviet republics exist. Telephones are more common west of the Urals than in the Asiatic parts of the Soviet Union and will likely remain so.[21]

Soviet Telephone Realities

What emerges from these statistical snapshots is a picture of a country where telephones are generally not a routine part of daily experience. The inadequacies of the telephone system itself helps account for this situation. A range of self-protective social attitudes is also involved. The penalties for unsanctioned communications are well understood by the rank-and-file. There is, for instance, a specific regulation prohibiting use of long-distance phone calls for "information hostile to the state."[22]

Soviet citizens are well aware of the government's ability to monitor phone calls, although they may not know the technical details. Most telephone systems throughout the world, in order to determine toll-call charges, use a relatively simple technology known as periodic pulse monitoring, which neither identifies the called number nor provides records of individual calls. The United States and the Soviet Union are among the few countries that use a more complex system—centralized automatic message accounting (CAMA). It can record individual calls, including the called and the calling number. CAMA's primary advantage in the United States is to provide records for income tax and other accounting needs. Soviet government motives are clearly different, centered as they are around monitoring and control. CAMA also has the advantage of allowing segregation of subscribers into individual classes. As a result, they can be assigned individual priorities in access to the network—an important point in a system where circuits are often overloaded.

These conditions lead to a built-in wariness by Soviet citizens in dealing with a communications device that, despite its undoubted advantages, could mean trouble. Office telephones are sometimes equipped with small locks to prevent unauthorized use when the individual responsible for the instrument is not around. Others are often locked up in a drawer or file cabinets when not in use. Much ordinary business is done over Soviet telephones, of course, but care is taken when conducting more sensitive conversations. This caution is expressed in a Moscow joke about Mikhail Gorbachev and Leonid Brezhnev. Brezhnev telephones Gorbachev from heaven and says he has some important information about how to run the country. "Tell me all about it," Gorbachev replies. "I'd like to, but I can't," Brezhnev says. "It's not telephone talk."

Telephone distribution is a hierarchical matter in the Soviet Union. The very top leadership has a profusion of phones, with six lines for a Central Committee member's desk reported as par. The highest level of telephone status is possession of an instrument known as the *vertushka,* which provides access to the private direct lines of the top leaders. These phones are tied to the Kremlin's private exchange, maintained by the Soviet secret police to avoid unauthorized tapping, presumably not including its own. An additional benefit for high officials is access to the *Ve-Che*, a high-frequency line for long-distance use that avoids the delays ordinary citizens put up with in making calls.[23]

Beyond the top hierarchy, telephone availability drops dramatically. Instruments are assigned to managers and other professionals on a sliding scale based on rank. The presence of a single telephone on an individual's desk still speaks of authority. Despite the practice of assigning telephones on a priority basis to public enterprises, there are still government units without telephone service, particularly in rural areas. The Central Committee's 1985 decision on telecommunications sets out as a specific goal the initial provision of such service to state enterprises that currently have no (or minimal) telephone facilities. Specific mention is made of completing installation of phone service to *kolhkozi, sovkhozi,* and other agricultural enterprises by 1990. In equally vague terms, the plan describes goals for supplying telephones to all rural schools, medical clinics, stores, cultural centers, and other public facilities.[24]

Telephones for family use are limited, as noted earlier, largely to urban areas. Again distribution is selective, with a high proportion of instruments going to favored groups (for example, party officials and professionals). The major exception seems to be the widespread distribution of instruments to war veterans and to their widows—a point often stressed in Soviet official pronouncements about telephones. In his 1985 review of telephone expansion plans, Ministry of Communications official Aleshin said that telephone service to all "war and labor invalids" would be achieved in 1988. War veterans and "families with many children" would be fully served by 1990. The rest of the population will have to wait. Official figures suggest that there is a backlog of 10 million applications for phone service throughout the country. Based on 1984 interviews with Leningrad citizens, this translates into a five to seven-year waiting list for ordinary Soviet citizens. Aleshin also reports that the new planning goal is to reduce the waiting period for phone installation to "a maximum one-year term."[25]

The chronic shortage of personal telephones places heavy reliance on public telephones. Long lines are a common sight at telephone kiosks and at telephone offices where intercity calls are placed. Given the demand for such service, there is a particularly acute shortage of pay-phone facilities. One Soviet commentary in 1985 placed the number of pay phones nationally at 260,000 instruments. The figure cited in the announcement of the annual production of such instruments was 10,000—a statistic that suggests that new production might not cover the replacement of present pay phones taken out of service because of obsolescence, damage, or other reasons.

Making a long-distance call is often a tedious chore. A June 1985 Moscow domestic radio report, reviewing telephone service in the Moscow oblast, said it can take hours "or even days" to complete an intercity call. Only 45 percent of phone subscribers in the oblast have access to automated long-distance dialing facilities, the report noted.[26]

Another barrier for Soviet telephone users is a lack of subscriber directories. A 1973 edition of 50,000 copies of a 4-volume Moscow telephone directory reportedly disappeared immediately. In the absence of standard phone books or directory assistance, the pragmatic solution for Soviet telephone users is to develop personal phone lists; making phone calls outside one's private circle is difficult. Government offices and other institutions are, by and large, impenetrable by telephone for ordinary citizens.

International telephone calling is also an exotic activity for most Soviet citizens. Despite its size and political importance, the USSR is essentially isolated from the telecommunications systems of the rest of the world. This isolation became an issue during international negotiations in the mid-1960s when plans for the Intelsat global satellite communications network were being developed. The network was set up as a consortium owned by the participating countries, with ownership shares determined by each nation's actual use of the network. The Soviet government was routinely invited to join the consortium, but refused. The refusal was based in part on the fact that Soviet ownership participation would be less than 1 percent. The Soviet government proceeded to develop its own satellite network, Intersputnik, whose membership is limited to the 14 socialist-bloc countries, compared with Intelsat's 113-nation membership. The USSR is, however, heavily dependent on Intelsat facilities, with links through two earth stations under special provisions for nonmembers of the consortium.[27]

Statistics on Soviet international telephone traffic are generally not available, except as vague percentages. Tom Stonier of Britain's University of Bradford has estimated that Soviet nondomestic traffic is one two-hundredths that of the United States. All international calls go through a central "gateway" in Moscow. International traffic in and out of the USSR is increasing slowly. In 1972, for example, AT&T had four telecommunications circuits linking the United States to the Soviet Union. Fifteen years later, in 1987, the figure is still less than 50 circuits, a miniscule number compared to the tens of thousands of circuits linking the United States and Western Europe.

As part of their showcase preparations for the 1980 Moscow Olympics, the Soviet government introduced automated direct-dial international telephony. The service was instantly popular, as it eliminated the long waits involved when operators were used. Although the primary users were Western embassies and businessmen, Soviet citizens—some of whom were dissidents—also took advantage of the new service to contact the "outside." In 1981, to discourage this trend, Soviet authorities doubled the price of a phone call to Western Europe to the equivalent of $4.50 per minute. This apparently did not discourage the calls. As a result, in 1982 the authorities cut back on the number of international circuits available and then virtually abolished the entire direct-dial service. Staff shortages and the need to repair equipment were cited as the reasons. The service has since been restored on a limited basis, primarily for Western users.[28]

One international telecommunications circuit that remains available, although little used, is the U.S.-Soviet "hotline" inaugurated in 1963. Despite the popular image of U.S. and Soviet leaders exchanging phone calls in a crisis (as satirized in the 1964 film "Dr. Strangelove"), the hotline actually involves teleprinters sending written messages from Washington in English and from Moscow in Russian.

Telephones and Computers

The Soviet telecommunications system must be further upgraded to handle the chores allotted it under the new Gorbachev high-tech initiatives. The problems begin with the national telecommunications infrastructure having been neglected for decades, except for military and government needs. Much of the new initiative must be focused on improving existing facilities rather than on developing new ones. The February 1985 Central Committee telecommunications decisions setting goals for automated facilities with a total capacity of 10 million telephone lines did not distinguish between new and replacement facilities.

Both qualitative and quantitative upgrading will be critical in Soviet plans for computer networking at the long-distance and the local levels. Current capabilities in this area are generally poor; the exceptions are in dedicated military and other high-security uses. According to William McHenry, a specialist in Soviet computers, the Ministry of Communications guarantees high-speed services up to 4,800 bits per second (bps) in its ordinary telecommunications service, although speeds of more than 2,400 bps are rarely reported anywhere.[29] Even the guaranteed number would be considered a very low performance level by Western standards.

Telecommunications planning in the USSR stresses the need for an all-digital high-data-rate system in the future, with computer-controlled switching centers. In planning the system, Soviet engineers are careful to conform to Western technical protocols to assure interconnectivity as well as the incorporation of advanced Western equipment. The network, when completed, will bring Soviet telephone service from a relatively primitive level to a standard that begins to match the needs of a modern industrial state. In the longer term, the measure of effectiveness will be whether the upgraded network can support a viable level of computer networking, linking many different levels of computers. Western experts, with only fragmentary information about the new system, are skeptical.

Another constraint on computer development is the Soviet industry's inability to produce much higher levels of advanced telecommunications equipment than it has done in the past. Pro-

duction turnaround time could be a serious limitation, given the
general neglect of this sector in past years. There are some indications that priority attention is being given to the problem. A 1985
Soviet press report described the opening in Latvia of a robotically
controlled assembly plant capable of meeting one-third of the
country's telephone instrument needs.

Other sectors have fallen behind. R.J. Raggett, editor of
Jane's Military Communications, has pointed out that production
of telecommunications cable, a basic need in the new expansion,
is far behind schedule because of poor planning.[30] It would be a
mistake, however, to underestimate Soviet capability to develop
an advanced telecommunications system. Western observers
acknowledge that the Soviet electronics industry has strong high-
tech telecommunications capabilities, although it will also have to
rely on Western imports. Soviet managers have considerable
access to a range of advanced Western products. In cases where
U.S. and NATO strategic export controls apply, they can usually
obtain what they want from non-NATO sources; one of their principal suppliers is Sweden's world-class electronics firm, L.M.
Ericsson.

Soviet planners will use a mix of telecommunications technologies in their expansion projects. High-capacity microwave and
cable networks will be important transmission links between the
new, automated switching centers. Fiber optic cable technology is
well advanced in the USSR and is being installed in small systems.
One curious aspect of Soviet planning to date has been the relatively limited use of the domestic satellite network for general
telecommunications beyond television transmission. Satellites are
a natural telecommunications link in the USSR, given the difficulties involved in extending terrestrial transmission lines in remote
areas and the geographic spread of the country, which covers 11
time zones.

Domestic Satellite Connection

The USSR has, moreover, an extensive domestic satellite system
in place. In line with the general secretiveness about communications facilities, information about the network is sparse and often

contradictory. Keeping the technical characteristics and operating uses of the system totally hidden is difficult because the satellites can be monitored from outside the country. This vulnerability is probably one reason why more extensive use of the system for telecommunications purposes is not made. The exception is transmission of television programs and other relatively public uses. Satellites also transmit the contents of the national party newspaper, *Pravda,* to printing plants across the country.

Civilian telephone, data, and other specialized telecommunications services seem to be a relatively small part of Soviet satellite traffic. In part, this reflects the limited intercity traffic in these services. Most long-distance telephone calling is actually short-distance; only 2 percent of all calls exceed 1,200 miles, according to Soviet statistics. Intercity telephone traffic is about 2 billion calls annually—roughly eight calls per capita per year. By comparison, a similar number of calls are made in the United States in less than two weeks. Another difficulty is that terrestial telecommunications facilities in the remote areas that could be effectively served by satellites are technologically primitive, causing difficulties in establishing working links to the satellites. By and large, Soviet domestic communications satellites themselves are not as technically advanced as Western models. They tend to have less circuit capacity and fewer capabilities for advanced telecommunications uses than counterpart facilities in the West.

To what degree the network is reserved for military and other strategic government uses is not clear. The communications satellite program is managed by MINSVIAZ, the civilian Ministry of Communications. Most satellite equipment is produced in defense production facilities controlled by the Military Industrial Commission (VPK) of the presidium of the Council of Ministers. One indication that the Soviet government may be trying to improve the operation of its nonmilitary space program, including communication satellites, was the establishment in 1985 of *Glavcosmos,* a national civil space organization roughly comparable to the U.S. National Aeronautics and Space Administration (NASA).[31]

In short, Soviet planners face strong challenges in upgrading the national telecommunications system, whether by satellites or other means. The optimistic goals set by central planners will slip.

There is no reason to doubt, however, that the USSR will have an adequate high-capacity telecommunications network by the end of this century, one that will be roughly comparable to current technical capabilities in Western countries.

Improved telephone service will be one of the more obvious benefits of the new system. The USSR will begin to achieve widespread telephone service a quarter of a century after every other industrialized country. Many of the economic and social benefits will be measurable (for example, greater industrial efficiency and better access to medical services). Less calculable will be the intangible social effects. Expanded telecommunications can have a positive impact on the overall quality of life for ordinary citizens in the Soviet Union. The wider availability of telephones in particular will, as a result, be a key element in assessing Soviet political and social development in the coming years.

For the present, the expanded telecommunications network is designed primarily to serve industrial, military, and government needs. The degree to which this improves efficiency will depend in large part on the constraints that Soviet authorities place on computer networking. The indicators point to continued limited access in ways that maintain many of the essentials of centralized controls. The price paid for these limitations will be forfeiting the full capabilities of computer systems in resolving economic deficiencies. To get a better view of how the Soviet leadership will handle this dilemma, the evolution of current Soviet computers and their use will be reviewed next.

3

Computers: Closing the Gap?

Computerization is perhaps the most important aspect of Mikhail Gorbachev's modernization program. It is at the center of the current Soviet high-technology initiatives. Ideologically, it fits comfortably into official dogma about a scientific-technological revolution. Computers confirm Lenin's fascination with the concept of mechanical slaves, which would free the new socialist man from the drudgery of work in a fully communist society.

In domestic politics, computers and related facilities are a critical element in redeeming long-standing party promises to run the country more efficiently. Failure to deliver on these promises could cut short Gorbachev's tenure as the country's leader. Economically, his program to reverse recent productivity declines will require more intensive and efficient exploitation of resources, among them computing capacity. Internationally, the USSR's ability to deal with mass computerization will affect the country's future over a wide range of issues, from trade to strategic defense to the prospect of a slow but steady erosion of the ruling party's domestic information monopoly.

There is a persistent tendency in the West to downgrade the computer capabilities of the Soviets. It is easy enough to document their failings and to be lulled by estimates that the USSR trails other industrialized countries in computer applications. Nevertheless, the USSR is one of only three countries (the others being the United States and Japan) with a full range of computer capabilities, from research and development (R&D) to applications. It has, moreover, a large installed computer base. The estimates by Western analysts vary widely, with general agreement that there are at least 30,000 mainframes and 70,000 smaller computers.[32]

From Stalin to Gorbachev

In their drive for more effective computerization, Soviet planners must reverse policies and practices that have hampered this sector for more than 40 years. Before Stalin's death in 1953, computer research was held back by the dictator's paranoid fears of a technology that threatened his control over Soviet society. One result was to divert the country's strong resources in mathematics and engineering to disciplines other than computer development.

By the time these Stalinist barriers were lifted in the mid-1950s, the USSR was far behind the West in both research and application of computer technology. This, in turn, led to a policy dilemma centered around the long-standing goal of achieving a high degree of national self-sufficiency in critical industrial and technical sectors. Early in their computer activities, Soviet planners adopted an ambivalent approach. While paying lip service to self-sufficiency, they relied heavily on copied Western technology in an effort to catch up.

The first large-scale production generation of upwardly compatible Soviet mainframes was based on IBM 360 technology, developed in the 1960s. The net effect was to limit, from the outset, the potentially innovative R&D efforts of Soviet computer designers. The decision to replicate Western technology was based on a desire to leapfrog the country's computer-development lag by assimilating proven equipment and its extensive software library. Efforts were focused either on buying Western machines outright or copying them for local production. In either case, domestic design efforts were given lesser attention.

In general, Soviet manufacturing style is not geared to continuing innovation. The standard practice has been to freeze production runs on computers and other equipment in an effort to achieve long-run efficiencies. Applied to computer production, this further limited any chances for matching the rapid progress being made in Western products, particularly after the large-scale introduction of microchip technology in the early 1970s. Western policies to limit transfer of high-technology to the USSR, although only partially effective, further complicated Soviet efforts to catch up.[33]

Another inhibiting factor has been the continuing lack of a clear locus of responsibility for the design and manufacture of computer products. In recent years, overall computer policy coordination was assigned to the State Committee for Computers and

Informatics. Whether the committee can, in fact, bring order to these sectors remains to be seen.[34] With the Soviet Academy of Sciences, at least six individual ministries and numerous subdivisions have been involved in the design, manufacture, allocation, and servicing of computers. The result has been a history of poor coordination and redundant efforts. Such inefficiencies have been compounded by Soviet efforts to assign computer-production tasks—under the rubric of the international socialist division of labor—to its East European client states. Operating under the Soviet-dominated Council for Economic Mutual Assistance (CEMA), regional cooperation in this sector dates from 1971, with the first joint production of components for the mainframe computer modeled on the IBM 360 series. The results undoubtedly helped strengthen computer capabilities within the CEMA region. However, the difficulties were considerable in both technical and management coordination among the national industries involved in meeting requirements for compatible jointly produced components.

Meanwhile, the disparity in computer technology and applications between the West and the Soviet Union remains high. According to Georgetown University Professor William McHenry, in 1983 only 7 percent of all Soviet enterprises (the equivalent of industrial plants in the United States) possessed mainframe computer management systems. Further evidence of a resource disparity is that in the same year only one-third of large enterprises (those having more than 800 workers) possessed mainframes, and their mean daily use was only about 13 hours.[35] At the same time, Western observers have reported on examples of increased efficiency in some enterprises where computers have been employed intensively for production planning and control.

When Mikhail Gorbachev became party general secretary in March 1985, he made clear his intention to press for a computer-based reformation of the Soviet economy. The task may turn out to be more difficult than he anticipated.

It is still too soon for even conditional judgments on the impact of his computerization proposals. These early years have been marked by much rhetorical whip-cracking, followed by relatively timid actions. There are, moreover, increasing indications

of the difficulties the Gorbachev planners face in implementing
their high-tech hopes. The evidence suggests major problems in
dealing with tough decisions in such areas as productivity, innovation, and management. The changes made so far have not
improved the economic outlook substantially. They have, however, been sufficiently effective to be seen as a threat to comfort-
able, long-standing practices by large sections of the Soviet
bureaucracy, particularly after the June 1987 economic restructuring policies were promulgated.

Despite these difficulties, the Gorbachev initiatives toward a
less rigidly controlled economy are relevant to the government's
computerization program. Nevertheless, the emphasis still
remains largely on top-down control, which is evident in the 1986
creation of a new set of superministries that are essentially amal-
gamations of older agencies. The machine-building ministry,
responsible for a large portion of Soviet computer and robotics
production, has been reorganized in this manner. This party-
knows-best approach to planning is, in effect, an intensification of
the strategies that have been inadequate in similiar attempts to
strengthen high-tech performance in past years.

The net result will be a sort of high-tech muddling through in
the coming years. A great deal of money and other resources will
be invested in computer-based facilities with mixed results. The
outcome, in any event, will be a significant upgrading of Soviet
computer capabilities by the mid-1990s. The main pressure to
perform will come from the need to check, and eventually
improve, the flat economic performance of recent years. A secondary pressure will be to narrow the technological gap with the
West, in part for trade purposes and also to assure high-tech par-
ity or better in strategic military areas.

In summary, Soviet planners still face major obstacles in their
computer expansion project. Old policies and practices must be
revised, and new ones adopted. Major changes are needed in at
least six areas: (1) research and development, (2) production
capabilities, (3) applications, (4) networking, (5) databases, and
(6) training. It is useful to look at the opportunities and barriers
Soviet planners face in each of these areas.

Opportunities and Barriers

Research and Development

As noted earlier, the Soviet Union has pursued a double-track policy in high-tech R&D, including computers. At one level, considerable resources have been put into large and often overlapping domestic research facilities in the interest of national self-sufficiency. At another level, there is a heavy reliance on Western technology, legally or covertly obtained. Western equipment is acquired by the Soviets either for direct use or for the technology that supports it. Particularly in the latter case, industrial espionage is an important factor; there are continuing indications that high-tech electronics is at the top of the Soviet espionage shopping list.[36] Despite difficulties in adapting foreign technology to domestic needs, such illegal acquisitions offer a shortcut to narrowing the computer gap with the West.

As noted above, Soviet efforts to buy or steal Western technology have hindered the overall effort to develop a domestic computer industry. Innovation in computer technology, with the possible exception of parallel processing and artificial intelligence, remains relatively weak in the Soviet Union. Much of their computer technology since the early 1970s has relied on Western precedents. Given the new Gorbachev emphasis on developing stronger computer capabilities, this dependence on external technologies may begin to taper off, although stopgap acquisition of advanced Western technologies will be a factor for a long time to come.

Soviet commentaries on computers minimize this reliance on outside resources. The emphasis almost always is on national self-sufficiency, together with claims of the greater ability of communism to effectively exploit the advantages of computers. Given the continuing role Western science has played in the USSR's computer development, the claims are disingenuous at best. The USSR certainly has the basic capability to develop and carry out a national expansion of high-tech computer facilities without unduly depending on Western resources. At issue is the flexibility of the Soviet computer industry and how quickly it can signifi-

cantly upgrade production and technology without substantial
help from the West.

An important step toward promoting greater self-sufficiency
in research and development was the creation in 1985 of a new
division of the Academy of Sciences—the Department of Informatics, Computer Technology and Automation—under the leadership of Andrei Velikov. Its purpose is to spur research and development work on computers and related technologies. Velikov is a
leading proponent of the desktop personal computer and has
reportedly drafted a plan for the development of computer technology up to the year 2000.

Meanwhile, the gap in some critical technological areas, notably semiconductors, has been narrowed in recent years. Soviet
factories now produce reasonably reliable clones of Western
microchips in respectable numbers and have even sold them to
the West in limited quantities. The issue of technological self-reliance remains salient, however, as the new Gorbachev leadership
moves into expanded high-tech programs. The policy of parallel
dependence on both domestic and foreign technology will continue and with it the competing claims of self-reliance against
pragmatic acquisition of Western technology for immediate needs.

Production Capabilities

Will Soviet industry be able to handle the demands for stepped-up
production in computers and related resources? Official pronouncements suggest the difficulties involved. Anatoliy Aleksandrov, former president of the Soviet Academy of Sciences, has
acknowledged that planning rigidities and departmentalization are
slowing down the assimilation of new computer technologies by
industrial enterprises. "The mechanism of transition from scientific research to development and then to mass production needs
substantial improvement here," he has noted. "The complexity of
the organizational form in this instance delays matters considerably and prompts a number of participating enterprises to use any
enclave to avoid this work."[37]

The production of computers, like most production in the
Soviet Union, has been dominated by quotas and targets. This

may change in the next few years as the economic restructuring plans announced in June 1987 take effect. Nevertheless, there is a heavy legacy of bureaucratic mismanagement to overcome in the computer sector. The old system has resulted in a long history of bogus production figures, design stagnation, and shoddy quality control.

In July 1986, a Soviet official reported that components for personal computers come from a total of 30 organizations. The agency that coordinates the development of personal computers operates out of 17 separate locations in Moscow.[38] It is difficult to detail the extent to which this top-heavy bureaucracy hinders computer production. Numerous articles in Soviet journals discuss at great length the characteristics of Soviet computers. Little information, however, regarding the production techniques or quantities produced is available. Estimates both inside and outside the Soviet Union suggest that production lags behind goals set in the current five-year plan. The Soviet computer industry must cope with these problems as it shifts to increased production of the smaller desktop machines that now dominate the industry in the West.

Lags in R&D efforts described above and the mainframe mentality that dominated Soviet production and application of computers until 1980 have also contributed to production delays. The shift to more efficient management is apparently now under way, but not without considerable design and production difficulties. In particular, production and distribution of smaller computers will have to be significantly expanded.

Although various models of smaller desktop computers have been produced in the Soviet Union, production runs are still limited. Western observers have seen no hard evidence that any single Soviet personal computer model is being produced in quantities exceeding 3,000 units per year. At least one microcomputer, the BK 0010, is designed for personal use. The catch is, however, that although they are for sale, they are not widely available in Soviet stores. In addition, printers are not likely to be introduced for some time. The price of the BK 0010 microcomputer, about 800 rubles or the equivalent of about two months of average wages, makes it unaffordable for the average citizen.

Personal computers based on Western technologies have been adopted as models for desktop educational and scientific/technical applications in the USSR. The Agat, a functional copy of the Apple II, has been slated for wide use in schools. Prototype clones of the IBM-PC have also been produced, including the Soviet/Hungarian Janus and the Soviet/East German MMS-16.[39] Production and quality control difficulties have reportedly hindered production of even these relatively simple machines.

The current five-year plan (1986-1990) calls for the production of 1.1 million personal computers. About half of this production is scheduled to be placed in educational institutions. Whether these goals can be achieved remains to be seen. It has been estimated that in Soviet schools alone, it would take 1 million desktop PCs to carry out the planned literacy programs.[40]

The need to step up microcomputer production raises the question of whether Soviet planners will seek outside help. The most efficient assistance would come from Western sources. Soviet officials have declared that they are open to such prospects. In a January 1987 interview with a Western correspondent, the director of the Institute of Informatics Problems, Boris Naumov, said: "We are ready to cooperate with the West in science, in fundamental research, in production, and in the future generations of computers. We want to organize joint ventures in many fields, and as soon as possible."[41] Despite these assertions, significant East-West cooperation in the computer field has little precedent and does not seem forthcoming. The more likely prospect for Soviet planners is greater coordination of computer-related production with East European client states.

The East European Contribution. To this end, Soviet planners have made strong efforts to promote development and manufacture of components in East European nations that are CEMA members. In addition to increasing overall production capacity, this project has been a catalyst both in setting common computer standards within the Soviet bloc and in sharing technologies and production techniques.

CEMA cooperation in this sector dates back to 1971 when Hungarian production began on the IBM 360-compatible ES 1010 (unified) system. In 1972, the Soviets unveiled a similiar machine, the ES 1020. Several other analogs of this third-generation IBM family have subsequently been produced in the Soviet bloc. The ES series has been the workhorse of the CEMA mainframe effort. Large-scale serial production of mainframe computers has yet to progress past the IBM 360/370-series-compatible ES machines. Although hard numbers are generally unavailable, Western esti- mates are that some 70,000 ES series machines have been pro- duced.

In 1974, a joint CEMA program was inaugurated for produc- tion of SM (small system) components, including both micro- and minicomputers. The first SM computer, the S5-01, was unveiled a year later. It had the distinction of being an original Soviet design, independent of Western influence. It was intended primarily for industrial, automation, and scientific processes. The SM series did not remain independent of Western influence for long. Technology comparable to the Digital Equipment Corporation's PDP-11 family of minicomputers has since been incorporated in the SM produc- tion effort.

In the early 1980s, microprocessors modeled on Western designs, notably the Intel 8080 and the Motorola 6800, were assimilated into the SM program. Machines based on these micro- processors were then produced in configurations comparable to Western designs. CEMA versions of Western minicomputers and microprocessors remain less powerful and reliable than the origi- nals that they copy. Nonetheless, since the adoption of these Western technologies, the CEMA SM program has expanded signif- icantly. There are now reportedly more than 50 minicomputer models in serial production in the Eastern bloc, some in respect- able numbers.

Soviet literature suggests that SM series computers have been used extensively for process control/automation in industrial enterprises. Some models are being used for design activities and assorted basic management tasks such as production planning, maintainance scheduling, and inventory control. There have been reports, however, of systems being deactivated due to a shortage of the basic programming and servicing expertise necessary to make the machines perform properly. Use of SM computers for advanced planning, spreadsheet production, word processing, and other common minicomputer and more sophisticated desktop applications in the West has not been widely evidenced yet. Design and engineering remain the predominant Soviet SM applications.

There have been indications recently that CEMA countries have agreed to expand the Soviet-directed SM program for coordination of microcomputer production. This expansion underlines the role assigned desktop models in furthering the aims of the Gorbachev modernization program. The diffusion of microcomputers, especially in classrooms, is increasingly recognized as the most efficient way of promoting computer literacy, a key component in the modernization drive.

Among CEMA countries, the leaders in computer technology and production are East Germany, Hungary, and Czechoslovakia. Poland and Bulgaria are less important, and Romania verges on being a high-tech basket case. In accordance with the "socialist division of labor" principle, each country specializes in one or more component areas. East German enterprises lead the bloc's minicomputer production effort both qualitatively and quantitatively. Between 1980 and 1985, over 40,000 microcomputers were produced in East Germany, most based on copies of Western models.[42] The USSR may absorb as much as 60 percent of the output of this and other CEMA computer production.

Hungary, perhaps the most independent of the group, has a very respectable software production capability. In part, this reflects the policy of encouraging more private enterprises in this and other sectors. In 1985, Western firms reportedly bought as much as $5 million worth of Hungarian software. One such software package, M-PROLOG, has been adopted by Japanese engineers for use in their Fifth Generation computer project, attesting both to the package's quality and to the hard-currency trade orientation of the Hungarians. A number of small privately owned Hungarian companies also produce desktop microcomputers, mainly for domestic use.

The CEMA joint production program has been rather unpopular, however, with East European governments for several reasons. It requires the subordination of their domestic industries to Soviet enterprises, which limits their ability to become self-sufficient in this sector for reasons of economic autonomy and national prestige. Production of most components in each country barely meets domestic needs; exports to the USSR, therefore, hamper indigenous efforts to produce computers in respectable numbers. Trade in high-tech components would, moreover, be much more lucrative for Eastern Europeans if they could obtain hard currency, as opposed to rubles, for their products. As a result, although only Romania has officially refused to cooperate in the program, the other CEMA countries are not enthusiastic about the "international socialist division of labor" in computers and other high-tech industries.

Applications

Despite CEMA expansion efforts, the Soviet computer equipment industry lags behind the country's requirements in this sector. These deficiencies are acknowledged by Institute of Informatics Problems Director Boris Naumov: "Certainly we have some problems and these aren't simple ones. The biggest problem is that we do not have enough computers. It's not the design of the computer that is the main obstacle, but organizing the production. It's a problem of developing a modern industry in computers which can provide what the users want."[43] (See appendix 3 for the full text of Naumov's comments.)

As noted above, Soviet experience with computers has been limited largely to mainframe machine operations and minicomputer engineering and process control applications. This is changing as the country moves into wider applications of computers, following the Western example. Two examples deserve special mention. The first is Soviet experience with robotics and other aspects of computer-assisted design and computer-assisted manufacturing (CAD/CAM). The second is the modifications that Soviet planners have outlined for completing a national computer network, designed to be the world's largest—the All-Union System for the Collection and Processing of Information for Accounting, Planning and Management of the National Economy—and known by its acronym in Russian, OGAS.

The exact status of Soviet CAD/CAM efforts is unclear. It is fair to assume that the Soviet military gets priority usage of limited resources. Clearly, the most sophisticated Soviet military products—airplanes, missiles, and submarines in particular—are designed and produced with the aid of advanced computers. In the microelectronics field, however, where virtually all recent Western advances are dependent on civilian sector CAD, the Soviets seem to lag.

Computer-assisted manufacturing (CAM) is still in its infancy in the USSR. While journals and newspapers extol the increased efficiency brought about by automation and flexible manufacturing, relatively little evidence of it has been seen by Western observers. There are confirmed examples of Soviet enterprises where CAM has been implemented and is reportedly working well, particularly in the automotive industry, where plants designed and sometimes constructed by Western companies rely on large-scale automation. The Italian-built Lada plant in Togliatti, for example, uses many assembly-line robotics processes; the Kama River truck plant also uses Western automated assembly line technologies. These are still exceptions, however, to the standard, labor-intensive manufacturing practices in the Soviet Union. Large-scale automated manufacturing probably will not approach the level of Western applications for the foreseeable future.

Gorbachev is, in any event, giving priority to investment in robotics as part of overall expansion in the machine-building sector. By 1980, 14,000 industrial robots had been installed in domestic enterprises, according to Soviet sources. The official plan called for production of 14,300 industrial robots in 1985, with 100,000 more in place by 1990. Robotics of any sophistication are heavily dependent on microelectronics technology. Given Soviet difficulties in producing adequate microprocessor-based control systems, it appears unlikely that this goal will be met. Nevertheless, these Soviet efforts are important. The current five-year plan, calls for an 80-100 percent increase in investment in this sector. If flexible production techniques can be dispersed more widely under this increased capital allocation plan, the Soviets may make significant headway in their quest for technological modernization.

Computer-assisted manufacturing will not, however, improve overall economic performance unless it is carefully coordinated throughout all pertinent industrial sectors, beginning with those responsible for producing computers and their components. Such coordination depends heavily on the completion of OGAS.

Networking

In the early 1970s, Soviet planners proposed an automated management system to increase the efficiency of the centrally planned economy. As far back as the 1950s, they envisioned a giant computer-based national information network that would realize this goal. Ideologically, it would be the centerpiece of a new phase in the scientific-technological revolution. The key elements would be the automated systems of management (ASU) conveying information up from remote offices, factories, and other workplaces to Gosplan, the central planning agency in Moscow. The result would be, for the first time, the efficient coordination of the planning and operation of the entire Soviet economy.

This was the OGAS concept that was given initial approval at the Twenty-fourth Party Congress in 1971. The program called for a system of regional computer centers to be linked to the main planning organizations in Moscow and to the rings of local computer facilities grouped around them.

Over the past 15 years, these plans have been repeatedly trimmed back, in part because of technical failures and management resistance to change. The Soviet press has criticized the program, pointing out that project computers were being used only part-time and then primarily for such routine tasks as payroll calculations. Although a major OGAS goal has been to reduce labor costs through enhanced production coordination, Soviet statements have indicated that there had been only a 0.5 percent reduction in personnel as a result of the project. OGAS/ASU has undoubtedly brought some measure of efficiency to specific sectors. The results to date raise doubts, however, as to whether such centrally directed computer networking can contribute significantly to Soviet economic planning and efficiency.

Two factors are involved in these doubts. The first is the degree to which the OGAS network is being modified to accommodate new uses of small dispersed computers. The basic format of the network was approved in the early 1970s when mainframe computers were the norm. Computer networking in the West is now increasingly influenced by linking small computers to each other and to mainframes. Little evidence exists that Soviet patterns have adjusted to the prospect of the more flexible networks permitted by the smaller machines. Following the June 1987 decisions by the CPSU Central Committee on restructuring of Soviet industry, the pressure for greater decentralization of computer networks could increase. Soviet computer specialists have reported that they are developing programs for more flexible use of computers. The question is whether infrastructural and political constraints will continue to inhibit the widespread application of these more efficient uses.

The second point is even more fundamental to the eventual success or failure of Soviet computer networking. Assuming that managers can be convinced of the potential gains possible through effective computer management techniques, which is far from clear at this point, will they be allowed the flexibility to operate their computers in ways that improve economic performance?

In large part, the answer depends on the freedom to make decisions based on objective information. Computers can be powerful planning tools when they are programmed to deal with all the variables in a given problem. They are considerably less effective when any of these variables are removed or tampered with. This is true when, as has been the case in the Soviet economy, production targets are determined in advance by arbitrary methods. To let the computer set the target is to surrender the power of the central economic planners to the machine, which would be ideologically unacceptable. The economic reforms announced in June 1987 should have the effect of modifying these situations. Even if this occurs, the problem of reliable data remains. One of the purposes of the reforms is to end the practice whereby prices are fixed arbitrarily and not in any relation to market forces. A worker's wages have not been a measure of the worth of his job; the price of a product has little relationship to production cost or demand, and the costs assigned to investment capital are not indicative of its true economic value.

Constraints such as these have plagued the OGAS network system plans from the outset. In particular, efficient use of the networks has been hindered by local managerial resistance to computers, manipulation of data, and the technical difficulties involved in linking thousands of computers nationwide to Gosplan.

Some steps aimed at mitigating these problems have already been taken. Beginning in 1976, the focus of OGAS operations shifted from distribution of mainframe management information computer systems that were operating inefficiently to factory automation and process-control minicomputer systems less dependent on human inputs and long-distance networking capabilities. The wide dispersal of such automation and process-control systems was probably intended to provide the infrastructural base for the more efficient functioning of OGAS down the road. Enterprise, regional, and ministry level management information systems accounted for over 75 percent of all computer systems installed during the Ninth Five-Year Plan (1971-1976). For the Tenth Five-Year Plan ending in 1980, 73 percent of the systems installed were process-control systems for enterprise-level factory floor use.[44] There are indications that this trend has been maintained in recent years.

Database Expansion

The collection, storage, and distribution of computerized data is a critical element in Gorbachev's high-tech expansion plans. Although the emphasis is on data supporting the economic sector, the USSR is quite advanced in setting up a full range of data banks across all disciplines.

As with other information resources, administration of Soviet data banks is strongly centralized. A State System for Science and Technology Information (SSSTI) operates under the general management of the State Committee for Science and Technology. (See appendix 2 for a description of the SSSTI organization.) This structure assures control over the acquisition of information in all forms—print, graphics, and computer data—as well as control over its dissemination. The largest center in the system for processing such information is VINITI, the All-Union Institute for Science and Technology Information. According to Soviet statistics, VINITI annually processes 19,000 periodicals and serial publications, 200 invention descriptions, and 10,000 books. Authorized users can subscribe to more than 80 VINITI data base files, which include bibliographic descriptions, key words, and abstracts.[45]

In April 1987, Soviet media reported the existence of a semi-independent data bank in Moscow that uses computers to sell information to state organizations and private customers. Headed by a professional programmer, a staff of nine people provides customers with access to what *Izvestia* called a "bank of ideas and people." The newspaper noted that the center, called "Ornament," is an "intermediary office," the only one of its kind in the Soviet Union. The center appears to represent an experiment based on a Hungarian model of scientific-technological cooperatives. Potentially the center may signal further attempts to combine more flexible mechanisms with high technology sectors in ways that improve creativity, productivity, and overall quality. This early experiment is a far cry, however from providing uncontrolled access to information and computer technology. Ornament is dependent on the state for credits, office space, and the booking of orders; apparently the data bank is located on a state-controlled computer. Moreover, the Ornament center operates under the guardianship of one of the district committees of the Moscow Komsomol.[46]

As noted earlier, networking in the Soviet Union is hampered by the poor quality of telephone lines. Transmission speed capabilities in particular are severely limited. This contributes to the relative lack of remotely accessible data banks in the USSR. Without reasonably sophisticated telecommunications networking, Soviet planners will be constrained in establishing more efficient national data bases.

Nevertheless, efficient networks have been established in the Soviet Union. The Moscow savings bank is said to have a network linking as many as 3,000 remote computer terminals. Networks have also been established to handle theater and ballet tickets and

hotel and train reservations. There are extensive networks servicing the police, armed forces, and KGB (including its customs and
border control branches). Each of these internal security networks exchange information via high-quality dedicated telephone
lines (not unlike the *Ve Che* described in Chapter 2) and are inac-
cessible to the public.

ACADEMNET, a computer network linking remote branches
of the Soviet Academy of Sciences, is a new but potentially important addition to the Soviet networking pattern. Western analysts
of the Soviet scientific establishment point out that scientific
research results and findings are generally distributed at a tedious
pace if at all. ACADEMNET is an attempt to address this short-
coming. Set up in 1979, it now links computers in scientific centers in Moscow, Leningrad, Riga, and Novosibirsk, making on-line
exchanges of information available. As it expands in the scientific
community, ACADEMNET could be a boon for both computer
R&D efforts and for Soviet networking in general.

The largest proportion of data-based information in the SSSTI
network is from Soviet sources. However, statistics provided by
Soviet authorities mask the extensive collection and distribution
of information from foreign sources. The USSR has reciprocal
arrangements for exchanging data with a large number of Western
institutions; in 1983, Soviet officials announced that data in five of
its large documentation centers would be made available to foreign users. Implementation has been slow, in part because much
of the data in Soviet computers is in Russian—a formidable barrier when one considers that most specialized data transmitted
internationally is in English.[47]

The Soviets are not, for the present, significant players in the
burgeoning field of international data trade—a sector where the
United States holds a commanding lead. Only one Soviet bloc
country, Poland, publishes annual trade statistics on information
services, and the level of its activities is very low. By extrapolating
information from other sources, a 1986 United Nations study provides rough figures on product-related data services in all CEMA
countries. The USSR ranks as the leading importer and the lowest
exporter among the six countries.[48]

Thus, international data flow is largely from West to East. It is supported by the extensive SSSTI program, coordinated through the National Center for Automated Data Exchange with Foreign Computer Networks and Data Banks (NCADE). The center serves as a control for all data exchanged between Western and Soviet agencies. The monitoring and control function is clear-cut; there are no direct data exchanges between Soviet and Western institutions.

Acquiring Foreign Data. The data acquisition system operated by NCADE raises important questions of technology transfer with the Soviet Union and other communist countries. In a very real sense, it is part of the fat Russian/thin Russian debate that runs through Western arguments about Soviet modernization. To what degree should the West help the USSR make up for its database deficiencies? The answers are reasonably clear (particularly among NATO nations) in dealing with sensitive data that affect the prospects of leading-edge Soviet military technology. There is considerably less unanimity, in policy and actions, when the issue shifts to the area of what in the West are considered normal data flows.

The issue was highlighted in 1982 when the U.S. government withdrew its support from a Vienna-based research organization set up in the early seventies as a détente project to encourage East-West technological cooperation. The International Institute for Applied Systems Analysis (IIASA) was supported primarily by the U.S. and Soviet governments to sponsor long-range studies on energy, food supply, environment, and other international problems. The cooperative project began to falter with charges that Soviet officials had used the institute's computers to retrieve sensitive military information from data banks in Britain and the United States. Both the U.S. and British governments withdrew their financial support for the institute. U.S. participation, which had been managed by the National Academy of Sciences, was continued at a reduced level by the Boston-based American Academy of Arts and Sciences.[49]

The difficulties of restricting any kinds of data stored in publicly available data bases has been documented extensively. One 1986 study by Dr. Jorg Becker of West Germany's Marburg University shows a sustained growth in data transfer to Soviet and other Eastern-bloc institutions, with particular emphasis on economic and technical data. The Becker study gives details on how West German data organizations serve as legal transmission points between Western data bases and customers in the CEMA area. In particular, Becker documents the limitations of the present control systems. Among the examples he cites are U.S. government-owned data bases on energy, aerospace, and foreign trade opportunities, which are licensed for access in the United States only. Denying U.S. commercial data purveyors the right to export such information may be a hollow exercise. There are, Becker notes, more than 350 branches of East European banks, trading firms, and other companies operating in Western Europe and the United States that need only to arrange for local delivery of data bases on the forbidden-export list. "From a technical perspective, the flow of data between East and West to an increasing degree is uncontrollable," he concludes.[50]

Is there any compensatory advantage for the West in abetting this Soviet advantage? Specifically, does exposing the Soviet professionals to Western data make any difference in softening their attitudes about the strict information environment within their own country? Any short-term hopes that such exposure will make a difference would be naive. Nevertheless, data flow from the West is beginning to emerge as a factor in the volatile mix of glasnost and high-tech expansion in the Gorbachev era.

Training a New Generation

Mikhail Gorbachev's success at creating a computer-intensive environment will depend on more than his ability to deal with the production and application problems addressed above. Another challenge is to train a new generation of computer-literate Soviet citizens who can operate the machines efficiently once they are produced. Given the scope of his plans, this will involve tens of millions of men and women, most of whom are now children. Any discussion of the political risk to the party's controls over communications and information involves the question of whether a critical mass of such computer-literate individuals will be developed in the coming years.

The Soviets have begun to implement such a training program. In September 1985, a new subject was added to the Soviet high-school curriculum entitled "The Fundamentals of Information Science and Computer Technology." Designed by Andrei Ershov of the Soviet Academy of Sciences, the new course is meant to familiarize Soviet schoolchildren with computers and their capabilities. Ershov described his vision of the computer's future in a 1986 *Business Week* interview: "We hope that the use of computers in education will whet the general appetite for technology. Children entering college in two years will be clamoring for computers. Once computers start spreading through the colleges, the production sector will be asking for personal computers."[51]

His vision is tempered, however, by the fact that computer access will be restricted to government-approved applications. In a 1985 *Pravda* article, Ershov acknowledged the built-in limitations of his program: "The task of introducing electronic computers into the school, and the approaches to its solution are emerging without precedent in history and must be carried out taking full account of our social system, its realities, and its cultural and social traditions." The realities he refers to clearly do not include the prospect of unfettered access to the full range of information resources.

In an earlier *Izvestia* article entitled "Man and Computer," Ershov underscored this point: "Programmers acquire a special knowledge of the information entrusted to them and the mechanism of its use. That is why they are confronted with a most serious ethical problem in its full blown form—namely, how not to abuse this professional knowledge."[52] Such comments reflect official concerns about the dangers of expanding computer literacy in Soviet schools. Nonetheless, the computer literacy program represents a potentially important commitment to furthering Soviet high-tech development. High school students now studying computers will eventually enter a work environment where computerization will be considerably more advanced than it is now.

This is the main reason behind the Soviet goal of introducing at least one computer into all 64,000 high schools by 1990. The original goal of a million classroom computers by that date, announced in 1984, was first halved and then scrapped for the more modest plan. There is, in fact, very little chance that even the most recently revised goal will be realized on schedule. The exact parameters of the new computer curriculum have yet to be defined. For the first year of the program (1985-1986) the plan called for ninth graders to have 34 hours of theoretical instruction. Tenth graders, or seniors, were scheduled to receive 68 hours of textbook instruction.

In theory, every Soviet student at the same level studies the same subject material on any given day. The new curriculum is being taught on a more flexible schedule, using two different textbooks. One is designed for purely theoretical instruction, to be used without hands-on computer practice. The other book, printed in significantly fewer copies, is designed for those students who will have access to computers. For the most part, this latter category of students will likely be those in elite schools that enroll children of top officials—the party, military, and professional "nomenklatura." By and large, they are the students being groomed for leadership careers. Presumably, they can be trusted as a group not to abuse the power that they will gain through access to previously guarded information channels.

The plans for introducing computer training in high schools falter on the basic problem of very few schools having even a single machine. This predicament is a function of the Soviet inability to manufacture personal computers in any quantity. Only 1,131 Agats (an Apple II clone) were slated for introduction in high schools in 1985. The Soviets purchased 4,000 low-powered Japanese Yamaha personal computers in late 1984 to alleviate this embarassing deficiency. The continuing inability to supply even a minimal number of machines led the former president of the Soviet Academy of Sciences, Anatoliy Aleksandrov, to comment that the study of computer science without computers was akin to learning how to ride a bike without getting on one.

Other options for hands-on training are available. Soviet reports have described the creation of computer centers where facilities, although only on a limited basis, are made available to students. One such center in Moscow is said to serve 1,500 students, presumably not randomly culled from average high schools. Enterprises with computing facilities have similar programs, allowing students to use their machines in off-hours. Some "Kombinats," (teaching/production complexes providing students hands-on vocational training) also have "collective-use" computer centers.

In spite of these options for would-be computer users, the reality is that very few Soviet students will have direct experience with computers in their school years for the time being. Access to computers is limited at best. In the larger cities—Moscow, Leningrad, Kiev, Novosibirsk—a devoted student might seek out a collective-use center and flirt briefly with a computer. In more rural areas, however, the chances of getting computer time are severely limited and will likely remain so for a long time. "Training in computers is like swimming. The earlier one starts, the better," says Andrei Ershov. This observation, while undoubtedly true, has little relevance for the majority of Soviet students. Where will the new cadre of computer literates come from? The leadership of the Soviet Union has called for more computer specialists at all levels of government, the military, and the economic structure. Despite the expansive official declarations about mass computer literacy, the question remains whether Soviet leaders will in fact permit such a development.

The answer may lie in the way Soviet planners deal with sensitive professions. Talented and trusted students will be identified early for specialized training. In a revealing commentary, the journal *Sovietskaya Pedogogika (Soviet Education),* points out that microcomputer allocation priority will be given to the elite Voluntary Society for the Promotion of the Army, Air Force, and Navy (DOSAAF)—a further indication that the children of the USSR's political heavyweights, nominally the most trusted element of the society, are being groomed as the first generation of computer literates. They will receive the hands-on training and be responsible for furthering the careful imposition from above of computerization in the Soviet Union.

Nevertheless, the prospects for Soviet success in its computerization projects will depend eventually on the ability to prepare millions of citizens for the new information-intensive economy. It is more than a pedagogical problem. It also raises critical questions about the effect that such a trained force will have on the political and social environment in the USSR. Will the new computer literacy result in a generation of more efficient compliant workers, content to remain within the bounds of a new kind of technocratic totalitarianism? Or will it lead to an erosion of the pattern of party controls that has marked the Soviet experience for over 60 years? These prospects will be examined in the next chapter.

4

The Future of Communications
in the USSR

Three questions must be asked about the future course of Mikhail
Gorbachev's high-tech initiatives in communications and information.

How successful will Gorbachev and his planners be in applying computers and related resources to the revitalization of the
Soviet economy?

What will be the political and social impact of any large-scale
expansion of telecommunications and information facilities within
a limited glasnost environment?

What effect will these expanded resources have on the USSR's
international influence in general and on the East-West strategic
balance in particular?

At this early stage, two trends seem clear. First, the Gorbachev initiatives are a serious attempt to upgrade Soviet communications and information facilities. These resources are essential
elements in the new industrial strategy. A half-hearted effort in
applying them will severely limit the rest of the economic revitalization program. Soviet managers have the basic research and
industrial capabilities to support major expansion in these sectors.
Barring some monumental mistakes, the coming decade should
see a significant improvement in telecommunications and other
computer-related resources in ways that can improve economic
performance and, by definition, military capabilities.

Second, the Kremlin leadership plans to deal with these
expanded technologies in a very different way from the West's
experience. The Western approach has been to encourage rapid
diffusion of computer resources at all levels of society. The USSR's
strategy is to continue to concentrate these resources primarily in
state military and industrial facilities. In attempting the first full-
scale computerization of a centrally planned economy, Soviet

efforts are defined by an ideology that sees computers and related facilities as validating the Marxist-Leninist view of a technologically efficient society.

This ideological factor has led to considerable speculation in the West about Soviet postindustrial patterns, ranging from predictions of a high-tech Orwellian society to suggestions that expanded communications resources will hasten the ending of the party dictatorship. Neither of these prospects is imminent, but there will be greater pressures in both directions. The eventual outcome of these pressures will have a profound effect on the Soviet future and, by extension, on the rest of the world.

The Economic Priority

The most immediate results of the new drive will be felt in the economic sector. Soviet planners are not starting from scratch; they have had more than 30 years of experience with computers and related resources. Although plans for the elaborate OGAS national network have been slow to materialize, large numbers of computer grids are being put in place. Martin Cave of Britain's Sussex University cites Soviet claims that over 3,000 individual network projects were implemented in the years 1983 and 1984.[53] The exact figures may be suspect, but there is little doubt that a considerable amount of computer-based networking is happening, primarily within and between governmental agencies and industrial enterprises.

Given the Soviet penchant for secrecy, it is hard to determine the exact extent of computer and telecommunications resources or plans for future expansion. All such details are classified information. What seems certain is that a muted debate is continuing over the ways in which these resources should be used. General agreement exists among the leadership on the importance of computer-based facilities in upgrading the economy. A hard-line group of the old guard still wants continued centralized control of these resources despite the economic restructuring reforms announced in June 1987. Other officials, generally closer to Gorbachev in outlook, are pressing for even more decentralization, with greater initiative given to local managers under more flexible guidelines from the center.

Improving computer and telecommunications facilities is only one part of the problem that planners face in reshaping the Soviet economy. Their chances for even limited success depend also upon the changes proposed in such key areas as pricing, distribution, and worker retraining. Many of the hard choices have not yet been made. In the short run, new resources will improve operations in specific enterprises. Their longer-term impact on the economy is more difficult to predict. Most Western observers believe that further reforms that encourage management initiative and liberalize traditional command-economy practices are vital to the exploitation of information technologies in ways that strengthen Soviet economic performance.

Given Soviet political realities, these changes will take place slowly. High-tech resources will be distributed to targeted sectors. Inefficiencies at the local level will continue until a broader base of technocratic managers is developed along with the necessary hardware to computerize their basic operations. In the best of circumstances, this distribution will not be completed before the mid-1990s. Nonetheless, an overall net improvement over the next two to three years is probable. The critical question is whether high-tech facilities whose most efficient economic potential is in the areas of decentralized management, production, and distribution can be introduced from the top down in all sectors of the economy. The answer is critical to the Gorbachev goal of making effective use of the new resources.

The Social Impact

These economic shifts are not taking place in a vacuum. As the West is learning, wrenching social and political adjustments are involved because mass computerization forces shifts in long-standing attitudes and practices. In their alternate version of a postindustrial society, Soviet leaders intend to channel these factors in ways that support their primary goal of strengthening the economic structure and, by extension, their own political power. There are indications that the Gorbachev initiatives have general public support, if only for their promise of some improvements in living standards.

These hoped-for changes focus on day-to-day concerns such as housing, food, and medical care. Improvements in telecommunications and information facilities are not, for the most part, high on personal agendas. (The one exception is the prospect of better telephone service.) The average Soviet citizen will begin to deal with expanded communications and information facilities in the workplace. At high-priority military and industrial installations, the changes may be dramatic. In other situations, the pace of change will be considerably slower. In any event, a subtle shift in the social environment is taking place. In its own way, the USSR is moving toward an information-based society.

The shift will be uneven. Some Western analysts have suggested that it will add a potent new dimension to the dissident movement within the USSR. Such a hope is, however, naive. The dissident movement is small, fragmented, and subject to continual harassment. Its members will be pointedly denied access to the new high-tech facilities, as they are now to telephones and copying machines. The primary beneficiaries of the expanded facilities will be a group who do not readily fit the dissident category. These are part of the large and growing cadre of young Soviet professionals. As noted in chapter 1, for the most part, they are career-oriented individuals who perceive their interests within the existing system. They are also the cream of the best-educated generation in Soviet history. Success or failure in the new high-tech programs will depend heavily on the competence, and support, of this group. Many Soviet professionals are already familiar with computers and related resources. This pool of computer-wise professionals will expand steadily as new facilities are put into place.

By and large, they can be expected to play by the rules laid down by the party and the government. Nevertheless some subtle changes can be expected. The new facilities will be used primarily for routine storage, processing, and transmission of information. Bright young professionals will also know that computers have powers that go beyond such ordinary tasks. These powers include the prospects for different kinds of networking such as personal electronic mail. Other computer capabilities also include the ability to simulate alternate realities—a potentially dangerous attribute in a society where there is one current version of "socialist reality." There will be no great rush to test the outer limits of computer power in this regard. The capabilities are there, nevertheless, for discrete computer simulations that challenge orthodox policies and actions. One of the more intriguing aspects of the new Soviet computerization is the degree to which such electronic heterodoxy will be practiced, either officially or otherwise.

The answer could lie partly in how seriously Gorbachev is willing to pursue his much-publicized glasnost policy. To date, his forays into this sensitive area have been limited and selective. Nevertheless, glasnost is a hopeful sign that the new leadership recognizes the need for easing long-standing restrictions on the availability of credible information in the mass media. To limit glasnost spillover into the growing numbers of computer channels in the coming years will, however, be increasingly difficult.

The government can be confident that the new generation of computer-conscious professionals will not use these networks for overt "anti-state activities." The potential threat to the party is less obvious and more long range: the development of an environment in which a growing professional class, in particular, will be dealing with increasing amounts of information. Here, rather than in traditional dissident patterns, is where a significant shift, involving an erosion of state controls over information and communications, can begin to take place. The change will be a subtle one, but one that can have a significant impact on the way the Soviet Union is run.

The eventual pattern may not, however, support Western hopes for the evolution of a more liberal, humane Soviet society. There is a certain predictability in how the current leadership is handling the transition to a postindustrial environment. By contrast, the expansion of a professional technocracy, supported by advanced computer-related facilities, could present a more troubling prospect for the West. Such a changing of the guard would not necessarily promote liberalization or relaxation of totalitarian controls. It could mean a shift from a power group that is incompetent to run an autarkic postindustrial society to another group that has the competence and the facilities to do so. In all probability, the changeover will be evolutionary rather than revolutionary. The effect, however, could be to strengthen the prospects for a more efficient totalitarian society, one potentially more threatening to the Western democracies.

There are other, more optimistic scenarios. The expansion of computer and telecommunications facilities could foster a more open environment, leading to the fragmentation of present control systems and the beginnings of a more productive, less repressive society. Increasing distribution of such high-tech resources is creating a middle class that is growing in size and power, a new factor in Soviet political dynamics. Jiri Pehe, a Soviet specialist at New York's Freedom House, believes that members of this emerging middle-class group "tend to be open to new ideas and do not easily accept monolithic doctrine. A key to the middle-class mentality is sophisticated consumption. In return for their labor, members of this professional class demand access to information, travel, and goods. In other words, their emphasis is on the quality of life."[54]

The Gorbachev glasnost campaign has had, in its initial stages, the effect of encouraging a limited but significant dialogue on these prospects. One of its most dramatic moments came during a Writers' Union Congress in June 1986, at which the issue was debated extensively. Equally important, a new slate of union officers sympathetic to further debate was installed. The achievement may be temporary, as has happened in similar situations in the past. It should not be discounted, however, as an indicator of deeper feelings among educated Soviet citizens for an easing of restrictions on their professional and personal lives.

The future direction of Soviet society cannot be simplified as a zero-sum choice between technocratic autarchy or some form of democratic socialism. The fact that both prospects must be seriously considered indicates how little we understand the dynamics of Soviet society. What groups will attempt to take advantage of this new situation? Will it be a new breed of technocrats who see an opportunity to advance their vision of a scientifically controlled society and replace old party dogmas? Or will it be a coming together of other forces with a vision of a more humane society?

For the present there is no visible challenge to the power of the ruling party in the USSR. Any erosion of this power will emerge very slowly. When it does, the new telecommunications and computer resources, together with the attitudes formed in a slightly more open environment, will play an important role. The prospect of significant attrition of the leadership's communications monopoly becomes a new factor in the formulation of the West's long-term strategy for dealing with the Soviet Union.

The Western Response

How can the Western democracies anticipate and deal with such a change? The subject is important enough to warrant a continuing look at the possibilities for influencing Soviet patterns in ways that can diffuse East-West tensions and nudge the USSR toward a more constructive political and economic role in the international community. The gradual easing of traditional restraints over communications and information, both within the country and with the rest of the world, would be a major element in any such development.

Western options for influencing the pace and direction of this development are limited. It is, however, useful to look at Western strategy in dealing with two components of the Gorbachev communications and information initiatives. The first is the possibility of cooperating with the Soviets in developing the new facilities. The second involves actions to influence the political and social impact of the new resources in ways that favor Western interests.

Proposals to help the Soviets expand their communication systems are based on the theory that, on balance, such development will benefit the West. The reasoning is that the new systems will reinforce and expand trends toward more open communications that have been started by the glasnost campaign and could eventually lead to a less repressive and less expansionist regime. The rationale for this belief is that concentration of Soviet resources on domestic reforms will reduce the leadership's interest in foreign adventures.

The best prospect for Western participation in the development of a Soviet information society is in the area of technology transfer. The Soviet leadership has made it clear that they are not willing to allot hard currency to large purchases of Western technology to the detriment of their own technological sectors. Government and scientific leaders have recently made overtures to Western industry to engage in joint ventures in these sectors. In particular, the Soviet leadership appears eager to invest in information technology hardware only insofar as it would enhance Soviet technological and manufacturing capabilities, thereby promoting greater self-sufficiency.

Modifying technology-transfer restrictions would be the most direct way in which the West might step up the pace of development of Soviet communications and information facilities. Whether or not this would benefit Western interests involves judgments about the effectiveness of the present level of restrictions, particularly the tight controls imposed by the U.S. government on its own exporters. A January 1987 report by an expert panel at the National Academy of Sciences called for a radical paring of the list of technologies protected by the United States and its allies. It said that, for many types of equipment, export restrictions are "no longer feasible or necessary," a position vigorously disputed by the U.S. Department of Defense. In addition to supporting continued strict controls on high-technology equipment, the Defense Department has advocated controls over what it calls "sensitive" unclassified information in U.S. data banks that is now available to all comers, including the Soviets. Over and above the domestic civil liberties aspect of the proposal, there is a practical question of whether such data can, in fact, be effectively shielded from the Soviets and other users. The ready availability of unclassified U.S. data from European middlemen (described in chapter 3) illustrates the limitations of such controls.

The essential point is that technology-transfer restrictions, however configured, can have a real, but limited effect on the pace at which the Soviet communications and information structure is expanded in the coming years. Soviet managers have adequate resources to do the job. That parts of the system will be built on a technical level somewhat lower than that of comparable Western systems is more or less irrelevant. As in the past, the Soviets are prepared to accept this disadvantage as the price for assuring that they are in control of the resources.

For the present and due to political and strategic security considerations, there is little immediate prospect of significant Western resources in building the new Soviet facilities. The West can, however, focus on the potential political and social impact of the new resources. As these resources expand, there will be heightened expectations about their potential effect on Soviet society overall and on political patterns in particular. The West must be prepared to deal with the social environmental shifts caused by the cumulative effects of glasnost and the new communications and information resources.

These trends will be difficult to measure. In part, this is due to the continuing problem of getting accurate information about domestic developments in the Soviet Union. Moreover, Western policymakers will be looking at these developments through the prism of their own experiences in coping with the social changes that computerization and advanced communications have brought. There are no precedents for measuring similiar developments in a totalitarian society.

In the short run, the current communications expansion in the USSR will tend to reinforce the party's political fortunes. The economy is already showing signs of benefiting from such reforms, as evidenced by apparent improvements in its 1986 gross national product. There will be a slow but discernible improvement in general living standards. The glasnost initiative will initially benefit the top leadership by defusing some of the general cynicism among the population as well as offering hope to intellectuals for a general lessening of bureaucratic controls over some of their activities. Gorbachev and his advisers appear confident that they will be able to manage these changes despite the risks involved. They believe that they can absorb a considerable amount of glasnost-type liberalization without any significant threat to the party's "leading role" authority.

The critical question is whether their assumptions will hold or whether there will be a significant erosion of the totalitarian pattern that has marked Soviet society for 70 years. Continued control of communications and information resources— the most sensitive area of party power—will be a major factor in determining the outcome. The transition is already under way with the limited glasnost campaign and the expansion of communications and information facilities.

How do the Western democracies deal with these developments in their relations with the USSR? Past attempts to influence Soviet domestic information patterns point up the difficulties involved—the refusal, for example, to implement the 1975 Helsinki Agreement provisions on more open information flows. Continued resistance to "outside interference" can be expected in the more complex information environment that will soon face Soviet leaders.

The West's options at this level are limited, but the ones that exist are important. The most important is direct information pressure—the continuation of policies adopted over 40 years ago. The primary resource continues to be radio broadcasting; the Voice of America, Radio Liberty, the BBC, and other around-the-clock transmissions are now integral parts of Soviet life, a fact that has been implicitly acknowledged by recent government decisions to reduce jamming of most foreign broadcasts. The existence of these alternate news and information resources becomes more critical now as the glasnost campaign begins to erode long-standing suppression of information from party-sanctioned channels. For Soviet citizens, foreign radio broadcasts provide a continuing gauge against which to measure Gorbachev's promise of glasnost.

Other information pressures are available. A new generation of technologies, such as videotape recorders and direct-broadcast satellite transmissions, expand the possibilities for reaching Soviet audiences. Access to Western data networks is broadening among managers and scientists, despite strict controls by Soviet authorities. As data networking expands within the USSR, computer hackers will attempt to break into Western systems.

These activities will have an impact in spite of their limited reach. The most effective influences the West can have, however, will be in demonstrating how its own information-rich, postindustrial societies can enhance personal and communal lives. Despite Soviet counterpropaganda, this message can eventually get through.[55]

New information resources can encourage Soviet citizens to consider alternatives to the future that has been laid out for them.

The resources could potentially empower them as the legitimacy and efficacy of Soviet governance becomes increasingly dependent on a generation of more sophisticated citizens who will operate the new resources. This can be a critical, new factor in East-West relations. In the meantime, Gorbachev's plans for expanding telecommunications and information resources will move ahead, balancing pragmatic economic needs against the threat of erosion of the party's information monopoly. The plans may turn out to be the most volatile miscalculation the new leadership has made in attempting to reverse Soviet economic decline on its own terms.

As Soviet specialist Loren Graham has remarked, "We may be about to learn that the Soviet system is not designed for the information age. If that is the case, it is going to be difficult for the USSR to maintain its pretensions as the world's second superpower in the decades ahead."[56] These are the stakes involved for the West in the changes taking place in Soviet telecommunications and information patterns under Mikhail Gorbachev's direction.

Appendix 1: Pravda *Announcement of the 1985 Decisions on Soviet Telecommunications Expansion*

The following is the full text of a February 26, 1985 *Pravda* story on decisions taken by the Soviet government to strengthen national telecommunications services through the year 2000.

At the CPSU Central Committee and the USSR Council of Ministers

On 23 January 1985 the CPSU Central Committee and the USSR Council of Ministers adopted a resolution, "On Measures to Strengthen the Material and Technical Base and to Develop Telephone Communication Services Provided for the Population in 1986-90 and the Period through the Year 2000," which is a constituent part of the comprehensive program for the development of consumer goods production and the services sphere 1986-2000, being drawn up in accordance with the 26th CPSU Congress decisions. The program provides for the satisfaction of the Soviet people's growing requirements for diverse goods and services, embracing an extensive range of all kinds of services for the population, including telephone communications, to be raised to a qualitatively new level.

The adopted resolution points out that the systematic development of communication means is being carried out in the country. At the same time, the population's requirements for telephone communication services are still not being fully met.

For the purpose of further strengthening the material and technical base and developing and enhancing the quality of telephone communication services provided for the population, the resolution instructs the USSR Ministry of Communications and union republic councils of ministers:

To elaborate and implement measures to develop the country's urban, rural, and intercity communications networks, measures which aim to meet more fully the population's requirement for telephone communication services;

To ensure in 1986-90 the planning, construction, and commissioning of automatic telephone exchanges in cities with a total capacity of 10 million numbers, the further development of the intercity telephone network, and the construction of the necessary buildings for automatic telephone exchanges. Targets have also been determined for commissioning the capacities of these communications means in 1991-2000;

To take measures to strengthen the material and technical base of construction and installation organizations of the USSR Ministry of Communications and the union republic ministries of communications in order to ensure the fulfillment of targets for the development of urban, rural, and intercity telephone communications;

To allocate, beginning in 1986, not less than 75 percent of newly commissioned telephones to the population;

To expand the network of urban, rural, and intercity pay telephones available to the population 24 hours a day, primarily in regions of new housing construction and in population centers where telephone communications are poorly developed, as well as in enterprises, establishments, and organizations with a view to increasing the number of intercity pay telephones 150-200 percent during 1986-90, and 500-600 percent by the year 2000;

In 1986-90 it is planned to have telephones in all medical establishments, schools, kindergartens, creches, Pioneer camps, trade enterprises, and enterprises for consumer and cultural services for the population in rural localities.

When more than 50 telephones are installed in enterprises, establishments, and organizations of the national economy, the construction of departmental automatic telephone exchanges is to be carried out, as a rule, using capital investments allocated to ministries and departments, with these exchanges being linked in the prescribed manner into the statewide telephone network.

To fulfill the planned program for the development of telephone communications the CPSU Central Committee and the USSR Council of Ministers have made it incumbent on the Ministry of Communications Equipment Industry, the Ministry of Electronics Industry, the Ministry of Radio Industry, and the Ministry of Electrical Equipment Industry to ensure in 1986-90 the production of equipment for urban, rural, and intercity automatic telephone exchanges, radio relay lines, pay telephones, transmission systems, and the necessary communications cables.

Construction ministries have been set the target of ensuring in 1986-90 and the period through the year 2000 the manufacture for the USSR Ministry of Communications and the union republic ministries of communications of the ferroconcrete products necessary to carry out the work on developing telephone communications envisaged in this resolution.

The USSR Gosplan is instructed to provide in draft 5-year and annual plans relating to the "communications" sector for ceilings on state capital investments for the fulfillment of the set targets, as well as providing for the allocation of construction machinery, excavators, crane trucks, bulldozers, dump trucks, and other equipment and materials to the USSR Ministry of Communications and to union republic councils of ministers for the construction and operation of the country's urban, rural, and intercity communications networks.

Union republic councils of ministers and the USSR Ministry of Communications are permitted to carry out in 1986-2000 the construction, enlargement, and modernization of the telephone communication projects outlined in the said resolution over and above the ceilings on state capital investments by using bank credits.

With a view to stepping up control over work on installing telephones in residential housing projects whose construction has been completed, it is deemed necessary to incorporate representatives of enterprises of the USSR Ministry of Communications and union republic ministries of communications in state acceptance commissions.

The All-Union Komsomol Central Committee proposal to send specialized detachments of students every year to work on the construction of telephone communication projects was adopted.

The planned measures will ensure a 60-70 percent growth in telephone communication services for the population in 1986-90 compared with the current 5-year plan, and as much as 40 percent growth by the year 2000—which will make it possible to meet the population's requirements for telephone communication services more fully and considerably enhance their efficiency and quality.

(Translated by Foreign Broadcast Information Service (FBIS), USSR National Affairs, Economic Developments, 1 March 1985.)

Appendix 2: The Organization of Soviet Information Systems and Resources

The following are excerpts from a *User Guide for the USSR Databases INION and VINITI and Telecommunications*, a 1986 joint publication of the United Nations Industrial Development Organization (UNIDO) and the International Institute for Applied Systems Analysis (IIASA).

Structure and Functions

The State System of Scientific and Technical Information (SSSTI) is the distributed hierarchical system for accumulation, processing, storing and distribution of documented information to support the fundamental and applied research, engineering and technical developments, industrial needs and economy management in the USSR.

The system is characterized by the:
—centralized and general management via the State Committee for Science and Technology;
—unified principles of operation and uniformed informational products and services;
—correspondence of the system structure (network of the All-Union, Central Economy Sectorial, Republican, Regional Intersectorial and lower-level institutions) to the structure of the Soviet economy management;
—centralization of processing and storing of source (primary) documents on its highest levels; and
—servicing of the end users via its lower-level institutions.

The SSSTI, as the figure illustrates, is composed of the following:
—10 All-Union Institutions for Scientific and Technical Information (STI);
—90 Central Intersectorial Institutions for STI;
—14 Republican (e.g. Ukrainian, Latvian, Armenian, etc.) Institutions for STI;
—113 Regional Intersectorial Institutions for STI;
—15,200 Scientific and Technical Libraries;

Figure 1 Structure of the USSR State System of Scientific and Technical Information

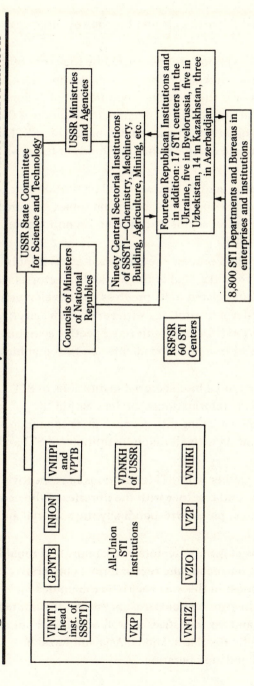

VINITI   All-Union Institute for Scientific and Technical Information—world scientific and technical information on natural, exact and applied sciences
GPNTB   State Public Scientific and Technical Library—databases on the location of domestic and foreign books and periodicals
INION   Institute for Scientific Information on Social Sciences—Soviet and foreign publications on social sciences
VNIIPI   All-Union Research Institute for Patent Information
VPTB   All-Union Technical Patent Library—domestic and foreign patent documentation
VKP   All-Union Books Chamber—all kinds of Soviet publications
VNTIZ   All-Union Scientific and Technical Information Center—non-published source documents (reports on research and development, dissertations, algorithms and programs)
VZIO   All-Union Center for Information on Equipment—catalogues and information on industrial equipment
VZP   All-Union Center for Translation—translation of scientific and technical literature and documents
VNIIKI   All-Union Research Institute for Technical Information, Classification and Coding—standards, technical norms and requirements, recommendations of international organizations on standardization
VDNKH   Permanent Exhibition of Soviet Economy Achievements—exposition of new developments and products of Soviet industry, agriculture and science.

—8,800 Informational Departments and Bureaus of enterprises and institutes.

The All-Union STI institutions are specialized by the types of the primary documental sources and according to specialization they accumulate, store and process the domestic and international flows of the scientific and technical literature and documents to produce the systematic informational files (databanks and databases) of SSSTI. These institutions accumulate and form the state funds of the primary documents.

Based on these products central intersectorial institutions for STI (CISISTI) publish and distribute information on topics specified for each scientific and technical sector by the State Committee for Science and Technology (SCST).

They also accumulate and process the published and non-published source documents from the field of the particular sector as well as other insector documents related to its progress and development. CISISTI supply the lower-level institutions with services on selective dissemination of information (SDI) and with retrospective searches as well as providing them with orginal documents and factographical data.

The republican and regional intersectorial institutions of STI (RISTI and RISISTI) provide informational services within the national republics and regions taking into account their economic specialization and cooperating with all-union institutions of STI and CISISTI.

CISISTI and RISTI together with STI institutions in respective enterprises and institutes, and together with the libraries of the economy sectors or republics compose correspondingly the sectorial and republican systems of STI.

Sectorial STI systems of generic sectors of economy and republican STI systems covering one economic region form a cooperative basis for regional STI unions. In this way the thematic unions for machine and building industries, agriculture, chemistry, the mining industry, metallurgy, oil and gas industries as well as regional unions of Caucasic republics, Baltic republics, Middle Asia and Kazakh republics were organized and are operating.

Primary Information Processed

There are several types of primary information processed by SSSTI: Soviet and foreign publications, books, monographs; reports on research and development activities; completed dissertations; patents; standards; catalogues of industrial products; and other documents.

The scientific and technical reference data on and from the above information sources are accumulated within SSSTI. They form the Soviet Reference Information Fund (RIF) which is the core of SSSTI. RIF now contains more than 2.2 billion documents (units of storage) with approximately three-quarters of them kept in STI departments and libraries of enterprises and institutions.

Scope of Information Services

The traditional services include: periodical informational publications; selective dissemination of information; and servicing the individual (non-regular) informational requests.

An important source of informational service is the periodical publications of STI institutions. The annual volume of these publications amounts to about four million pages, from which: 20% are bibliographical information; 53% are reference materials; 7% are express information; 8% are reviews; and the remainder are news on scientific and technical achievements, catalogues of industrial products.

The share of All-Union STI institutions comprises 63% of the total annual volume, with 28% and 9% going to CISISTI and RISTI respectively. The public distribution of the above-mentioned informational publications is arranged by centralized subscription via the All-Union agency *Soyuzpechat*, whose subscription catalogue includes about 3,000 titles of STI publications.

In addition, such CISISTI institutions as those on agriculture, building construction, and health-care function as All-Union informational centers, namely:

—All-Union Research Institute for Information and Technico-Economic Research in Agriculture (VNIITEISKH);

—All-Union Research Institute for Scientific Information on Building Construction and Architecture (VNIIIS);

—All-Union Research Institute for Medical and Medico-Technical Information (VNIIMI).

Selective dissemination of information (SDI) is the most widely used type of service by which the users get information about newly stored documents. The number of SDI users has reached 700,000; the number of stored SDI profiles exceeds 1.3 million. Annual servicing of the non-regular informational requests (answering user queries, preparing document collections on specified topics, etc.) includes on average answering seven million individual queries with a total volume of document copies distributed by this service exceeding 800 million pages.

Computer Systems

The existing SSSTI is based on the conventional technology of storing, processing and communication of scientific and technical information as well as on advanced procedures using computer networks and remote access to databanks. They are intended for the users of USSR and CMEA countries as well as those in other countries having access to each other's databanks on a reciprocal basis. The SSSTI is being steadily transformed into the State Automated System of STI (SASSTI). This current SSSTI development is based on: usage of computer and communication technology; introduction and operation of automated systems of STI in all national republics and for all economic sectors; and connecting these systems by the All-Union public data transmission system into the state network of the automated informational centers and the distributed databanks.

In 1979-80 a network of database producers was formed. It was started in 1973 by the first Soviet database producer POISK (in VNIIPI). In 1976 it was joined by VINITI. At the end of 1980 the network consisted of 13 centers.

Currently within SSSTI there are: 36 informational institutions operating as providers of the databases on magnetic tapes; 78 operational automated systems of STI (ASSTI) functioning as database operators; and computerized data retrieval service based on them and functioning in offline and online modes.

The latter is now available for remote users via telephone and telegraph lines to the databases on natural, technical and social sciences.

In the USSR the databanks are created within SSSTI on any level (in All-Union, republican, industrial sectorial, territorial institutions and information bureaus in various enterprises as well). Many research institutions of the USSR Academy of Sciences create databases in addition to those in SSSTI. These databases are accessible not only to Soviet users but also can be made available to foreign locations.

Before the end of 1986 the operational part of SASSTI will include All-Union, main sectorial (energy, chemistry, instrumentation, electrotechnology, building and agriculture) and six republican (Russian Federation, Ukraine, Byelorussia, Kazakhstan, Azerbaidjan and Armenia) informational systems.

Functionally, SASSTI will represent the system of regionally distributed, but interrelated informational centers which cooperate and utilize the same technological processes in joint processing, storing and dissemination of information as well as in creating and maintaining the united mass of reference data. By 1990 SASSTI will include all basic fields of Soviet and foreign science, technology and industry. It will be accessible via the state data transmission network interconnected with foreign networks and databanks.

Automated Data Exchange

The USSR National Center for Automated Data Exchange (NCADE) has an important role in the transmission of data. It functions as a Recognized Private Operating Agency (RPOA) under the Post and Telecommunications Administration (PTT) and provides users with the computerized data transmission services for reciprocal access to the informational and computational facilities in foreign countries and in the USSR.

Through NCADE Soviet users can have access to various foreign informational resources commercially available via TRANSPAC, IPSS, DATEX-P, SHARP, TELEPAC, FINPACK and others, and Soviet informational and computing facilities can be made accessible to foreign users.

NCADE takes part in the development of ACADEMNET, a joint information and computing network of the Soviet academic institutes. In this project NCADE operates as a communication node linking ACADEMNET subscribers with foreign networks.

The first part of ACADEMNET will be put in operation this year. It will link together several regional data communication nodes within the country and will facilitate the data exchange between the participating institutions via a packet-switched network. All hardware and software forming the basis of the ACADEMNET has been designed and manufactured in the USSR and other Council for Mutual Economic Assistance (CMEA) countries.

CMEA System for STI

SASSTI was created with the extensive cooperation of the CMEA countries. From the beginning it has been part of the International System of Scientific and Technical Information. At present specialized sectoral systems of STI on machine tools engineering, non-ferrous metallurgy, chemistry, building construction, electro-engineering, power engineering, agriculture, food industry and others are under development or being introduced. In operation are such specialized systems as those on patents, industrial catalogues and registration of serial publications. The leading organization in the development of ISSTI is the International Center for Scientific and Technical Information (MCNTI), Moscow created in 1969. It is especially active in developing the experimental data exchange network of CMEA countries.

In practical terms information exchange (access to SASSTI) is now arranged via the system of the national centers for automated data exchange of the Socialist countries. The USSR NCADE is one of them. It is connected by data links and information is exchanged with such CMEA national exchanges as: the Central Institute for Scientific and Technical Information in Sofia, Bulgaria; the Electrical Power Institute in Budapest, Hungary; the Central Institute for Documentation and Information in Berlin, GDR; the Institute for Documentation and Information in Havana, Cuba; the Institute of Computer Technique Fundamentals in Warsaw, Poland; and the Central Technical Basis in Prague, Czechoslovakia. In Mongolia and Vietnam national exchanges are now under preparation.

Appendix 3: Soviet Official's Views on National Computerization Progress

The following is the full text of an interview with Boris Naumov, director of the Institute of Informatics Problems in Moscow. Mr. Naumov's comments provide an interesting perspective on Soviet official thinking about the country's new computer initiatives. This article appeared in the March 15, 1987 issue of *Datamation* © 1987 and is reprinted here with the permission of the Cahners Publishing Company. The interview was conducted by the magazine's international editor, Paul Tate, and David Hebditch, a member of its advisory board.

Opening Moves

Boris Nikolaevich Naumov, the distinguished director of the Soviet Union's Institute of Informatics Problems, sits in his Moscow office and pounds his fist emphatically on his desk.

"We are ready to cooperate with the West in science, in fundamental research, in applications, in production, and in the future generations of computers. We want to organize joint ventures in many different fields, and as soon as possible. It depends on you, not on us. We are ready. Are you?"

Naumov pauses to let his heavily accented words sink in. He picked up much of his English during his time as a visiting professor on process control systems at MIT in the late '50s. A few years later he began the design and development of the USSR's strategic minicomputer line, the SM series. Now his status as an academician at the Soviet Academy of Sciences, as the head of an institute in the front line of the Soviet Union's mass computerization scheme, and as a leading figure in the Eastern Bloc's 11-nation research program into future generation systems makes him one of the grand masters of Soviet computing. . . .

His call for East-West cooperation, during an exclusive interview with DATAMATION in Moscow, reflects the new, highly publicized Gorbachev policy of openness, or *glasnost.*

"From my point of view," he continues, "we must progress in many different ways with this cooperation. We must feel it is profitable both from your side and our side. When I say profitable, I'm not just talking about money, but about it being a very useful thing for the progress of technology."

Naumov is not naive. He realizes that access to a massive and eager new market is very tempting to the West's business community. He also realizes that such an offer is highly contentious, since many in the U.S. believe that any increase in U.S.-Soviet dp trade will strengthen the USSR's military resources.

Naumov feels this view is misguided. "Maybe, if a company has a secret, then it must save it, and if a technology is used in rockets or something like that, then it is impossible to share it, but for other things, no problem. Take the pc. What is strategic about a personal computer?"

That is no longer just a Soviet view of the U.S. high-tech export controls with the Eastern Bloc. A recent report from the U.S. National Academy of Sciences says the consequence of stringent export controls for U.S. companies is lost business of around $9 billion a year, and the U.S. government is preparing to lower some barriers to East-West trade . . . .

Some forms of East-West cooperation may indeed benefit both sides. Most observers put the Soviets about five years behind the West in hardware. They are just moving into volume production on 16-bit pcs, 32-bit superminis, and multiprocessor mainframes running under operating systems similar to IBM's VS/VM. The software gap is narrower, particularly in operating systems and process and production control applications. Soviet scientists have been responsible for a number of important developments, from linear programming to some of the language compiler theories now being used in Japan's Fifth Generation Project. . . .

Where the Soviets have excelled is in the fields of computing science, application algorithms, and theory. What the Soviet Union lacks is an industry that can back up those theories with volume production—a point that Naumov readily admits.

Not Enough Computers

"Certainly we have some problems, and these aren't simple ones," he says. "The biggest problem is that we do not have enough computers.

It's not the design of the computer that is the main obstacle, but organizing the production. It's a problem of developing a modern industry in computers which can provide what the users want.

"For each area we are ready to have serious discussions with your companies and your people. That is why we are asking you if you are willing to cooperate with us at this time. We are prepared to join with you. If you are not prepared to join us, then excuse us please, but goodbye. We will survive without you.

"If in future we work by ourselves, like NEC does in Japan where its computers aren't compatible with anything, then it will produce very bad conditions for your businessmen. It will be impossible to sell to us. Those products will not be compatible with our computers.

"So, I propose that we organize an international institute for the standardization of future generation computer systems—to work together at a fundamental level. When we have got those standards, you will go back to your countries and build systems using your technology and we will go back to our country and build with our technology."

Naumov also proposes ventures for linking medical databases via satellites and pcs, for developing cheap and simple educational software and hardware, and for designing and developing integrated manufacturing systems.

Naumov isn't prepared to agree to just any type of venture, though. "I have had some proposals when companies want to organize joint ventures for producing old products. We must buy modern products, not old ones. These must have compatible software with our own, like Unix or something else we want to use, and have high-level interfaces for instrumentation. I have had a few cases when Americans have sold us very bad things—like an IBM XT [clone] (not from IBM; IBM always sold us very good products). These are very bad computers and they still don't work. Now we are not so stupid and in future we will not buy these.

"But we have bought computers from the Japanese and these are very good. We bought 4,000 Yamaha computers with a simple network for schools. They are very reliable and they are very cheap. I like the Japanese. They are very accurate in their technology and their business relations. But they have problems. When IBM wants to sell us IBM XTs for example, it is easy. But when we wanted to buy from the Japanese they had 10 times more trouble getting approval."

The widespread economic and social reforms rapidly being introduced in the Soviet Union by First Secretary Mikhail Gorbachev depend heavily on the mass use of computing technology to make them work. . . . The Soviet Union needs products fast. The USSR's current Five-Year Plan calls for 1.1 million microcomputers to be installed by 1990 and for production of all computers to be increased by 140% over the same period.

"We made many serious decisions at the 27th Congress," explains Naumov, referring to the Communist Party's meeting in Moscow in February 1986, "especially about how we must improve in the fields of informatics and computers and so on. It is one of the main directions that we must follow in our country.

"Maybe for us it was more important to apply computers as process control computers at first. At that time we did not use computers in office automation so much. Now we are using them for text editing, for spreadsheet calculations, for local information retrieval, and so on."

This "electronization and computerization of the national economy," as Naumov describes it, is being supported by a three-pronged policy: the creation of a stronger, independent Soviet dp industry; extending technical cooperation with other Eastern Bloc countries; and seeking stronger commercial and scientific links with the West.

"In many countries people are mistaken," he observes. "You think that it is only possible for our country to buy computers from the U.S. or from other Western countries. But you must understand that our country is a great country, like your country, and the first problem we must solve for our country is to improve our own industry. It's impossible, in any case, only to buy. We must have our own industry. This is the first way we are going ahead and we are doing so very actively. We have agreements with other socialist countries that have been given the highest priority."

Joint Projects Involved

Those Eastern Bloc accords involve joint projects among 11 socialist countries covering the production of the current ranges of mainframes, minis, and pcs. There are also links between the Academies of Science of these countries involving extensive and ambitious programs of joint research into future technologies such as AI software and computer architectures. These fall under the Eastern Bloc's Comprehensive Program of Scientific and Technological Progress to the Year 2000.

But for all the grand plans, Naumov concedes that some aspects of the Soviet technology industry are still weak: "We are only at the first phase of this development," he explains. With so much political attention being paid to the use of computers, however, he is confident that the existing industrial infrastructure can be quickly improved. As Naumov puts it, "It may take us a long time to harness the horse, but when we have, then we like to ride very fast. Look at our achievements in nuclear power—not Chernobyl!—and space technology."

Certainly, the Soviet computing industry has become increasingly independent. For example, Naumov revealed that he is now completing the design of a combined television and 16-bit computer, costing, he says, the same as a regular color tv, and destined for mass production later this year. Naumov explains, with one of his easy smiles, "Because Mr. Reagan restricted our relations in the field of computers, we have improved faster than we thought before. We're grateful to him."

Naumov continues in a more serious vein. "Many times, I hear people in the West say that we just copied DEC or IBM or so on. It's not true. It's impossible for us to have direct copies like that. IBM and our computers are quite different. Now we are going our own way."

Naumov's point here is significant. While Soviet component technology may be competent, it does not match the sophistication of that in the U.S. or Japan. To copy a U.S. machine, chip for chip or board for board, would be impossible. The Soviet DEC-like SM Series of minicomputers and the Soviet IBM 360-like ES mainframes have more in common with plug-compatible systems than direct copies. . . .

Yet Naumov admits that in the past these two major U.S. companies did provide a direction for Soviet hardware development. "Certainly, there was a time when we were working with the standards set by DEC and IBM, but we were prepared to pay for that," he says.

Naumov's reference is specifically to East-West discussions on licensing U.S. technology. "If you want just the technology then you must pay for it," he repeats, "and we wanted to pay DEC, for example, to use their standard. We had discussions with senior people and at that time it would have cost us between $5 million and $7 million to use the DEC standard in our circumstances. And our officials agreed. But after that, along came the bureaucrats and. . . ." He shrugs eloquently.

The result of that failure of the two superpowers to cut a licensing deal was that the Soviet Union became more active in developing its own range of DEC-like systems, the SM Series. There are some DEC systems that have entered the country via the so-called gray trade, which bypassed the export restrictions. . . . Nevertheless, most of the estimated 60,000 SM minis now installed, of which 40% are employed in process control tasks, were designed and built in the Soviet Union and other Eastern Bloc countries. That was Naumov's job until 1983.

Even More Strategic Role

Now his role as the head of the Institute of Informatics Problems (IPIAN) is even more strategic for the development of the Soviet dp industry. IPIAN employs around 900 computer specialists working in its Moscow headquarters and three other offices across the country. It is a part of the Soviet Academy of Sciences, which is represented on the newly formed State Committee for Computers and Informatics, the main policy-making body for computer use in the Soviet Union.

IPIAN has a wide brief. It is a research and consultancy group, assessing user needs and translating them into recommendations for new products and systems. Naumov explains, "Our institute is quite ifferent from other institutes because we do fundamental research and we are working on current problems. Our main direction is to work in the different fields of computing for mass applications, from personal computers to megaminis."

That covers three main areas: short-term product development in both hardware and software, free dp consultancy to the whole of the Soviet industrial and scientific community, and long-term research into new technologies.

Within those three areas are a number of other specific responsibilities. "It's impossible for our institute just to take only one problem," Naumov explains. "The main task is to understand what is necessary to develop effective applications—to feel, to understand the real problems, especially for our country, a socialist country. . . . The level of production today is also under our control. We must give advice—good advice—on how to improve it. We must also give technical advice on which foreign computers to buy."

Much of Naumov's current work is focused on personal computers. "In terms of the importance and the numbers of these machines," he says, "it is certainly a high priority in the Soviet Union. It's the cheapest technology, and it's more effective than larger systems.

"But we don't see the personal computer as a independent machine. It is impossible, from my point of view, to divide [minis and micros]. The division is the result of an American definition. We like to say simply that these are computers for mass use, for a very wide field of applications."

This is obviously one of Naumov's favorite topics and he carries on enthusiastically.

"That division was a strategic mistake of the policy for small computers in the West. If you consider the standard pc—I must be polite to IBM, because I like this company very much—but it is not possible to connect many things around the pc. Many of the interfaces are only there in principle. When you want to [share] it in bigger configurations for applications packages like a spreadsheet—Lotus 1-2-3 and so on—you can't.

"And it's also necessary to have a real-time operating system for pcs. But you don't have that. Only MS/DOS.

"But DEC always had systems designed to be used in big configurations with different types of operating systems, and now you are looking back to the DEC approach. They are rising in the field of technology because they are cheap and you can use their systems for any type of application. That was a strategic mistake of many American companies. At first they had some real success with pcs, but they did not think about the future in different fields of applications. That is my personal opinion."

Naumov's philosophy of strong integration and standardized multiuser small systems lies behind much of the development work at IPIAN. Naumov reveals that the institute is "working on new architectures for personal computers, pcs with local networks, different interfaces to link scientific, medical, and factory floor instruments to pcs, powerful server systems, and shared memory for mainframes and small computers."

Naumov is also working with other development groups in his capacity as the head of the Intersectoral Scientific and Technological Complex (ISTC) for Personal Computers. This is one of the organizational innovations that was introduced by Gorbachev in December 1985. It is designed to overcome the rigid structure of Soviet ministries that are responsible for specific vertical sectors of industry or society. By creating a cross-sector organization that will pull together all the country's specialists in one field, Gorbachev hopes to shortcut the decision-making process, help put theories into practice much faster, and pool valuable resources.

The ISTC's designers work on prototypes and then place manufacturing contracts with the ministries that offer the best deals on cost and quality. This Western-style competitive bidding for contracts is a new development for the Soviet system.

"It is a very interesting new forum," says Naumov. "We are the leading organization, and around us we have all the groups that are working in the field of personal computers. We are responsible for all technical matters for personal computers on many levels. We are preparing the programs, we are designing the operating software, and we are forecasting the number of pcs we will need."

Those forecasts suggest that after the first installation phase of 1.1 million pcs by 1990, the number of micros will triple over the following five years. This may not seem like much when compared with Western markets, but Naumov suggests that such direct comparisons are invalid.

"You see, this first million might be quite enough for our needs until 1990. In our planned system we know what sort of computers and how many of them we need for each industry. We will probably need only a few general purpose pc software packages, too—maybe

10 or 15 covering accounting, forecasting, text editing, graphics, data management, and so on. It is not like other countries where there is a market to sell to."

Strengthening Educational System

A top priority for the Soviet Union during the early stages of this micro revolution is the strengthening of its educational system. Naumov estimates that "a little less than half of our microcomputers are for education at the moment. Like in Lenin's time when education was the first problem, now educating people to use computers is our first problem."

There are already a number of computer schools in the country. Among the systems installed are simple networks of National Panasonic and Yamaha micros from Japan, conforming to the MSX standard for systems software and hardware. The first Moscow center serves 1,500 students aged 15 and 16 who each attend for one day a week over a period of two years. They learn some aspects of computer science and BASIC programming, and get some hands-on experience.

Naumov wants to take computing to much younger Soviet children. "We will develop very small, very cheap computers for children, maybe before they are of school age. The trouble is that I don't like many of the computer games in your countries. Mostly it's piff poff, piff poff. Sometimes I like to piff poff too, but in principle we must improve these games. They should be designed to improve the intellect, to improve knowledge in special fields and decision-making."

Naumov maintains that policy of easy-to-use but effective software when developing packages for other application areas. "You see, software must be simple. Then it must be effective. After that you can put the software into an organization very quickly. The software that is around now—like Lotus and Supercalc and so on—it is good, but it is only the very first stage."

He would like to combine the abilities of Western software companies with the work on "application algorithms" now being done in the Soviet Union. This brings Naumov back to the problems of setting up such cooperative ventures.

"I have said to many people from the West, to IBM, to many companies, 'Let us sign.' But they cannot. They must ask somebody."

Naumov holds a document, typed in Russian, above his head. "This is a copy of the Helsinki Accord, and I can show you what was agreed by the American president. It talks about cooperation in the computer field, telecommunications, and information technology. Look, it's page number 46 in Russian. And it was signed by the president of the United States. It means zero. I don't believe the signature of the United States—not in my field."

Of course, the Helsinki Accords, signed by President Ford and Leonid Brezhnev in 1975, cover many areas, notably human rights. While no country is above reproach, as pointed out by Helsinki Watch, the private monitoring group, the differences are "significant" between the Western countries and the Soviet Union and its satellites, which have committed the most egregious violations of the agreement.

The technology clauses are vague, referring to "possibilities for improving cooperation," but Naumov takes them very seriously. He stresses the difference between such accords and commercial deals. "When I have had relations with different private companies, when they signed something, they always gave me 100% or sold me what they promised. You see, in my field the president's signature means zero. The agreement was not fulfilled." Naumov believes part of the trouble is that "the responsibility to give the okay or not for technology trade lies not with the heads of the computer companies but with bureaucrats who don't know the difference between a bit and a byte."

In his view, these people stand in the way of genuine scientific and commercial cooperation—and of the natural links that govern the way societies interact, whatever their political persuasion. That is particularly bad for the scientific community, which has always had something of an international ethic, one that has most of the time managed to overcome political boundaries.

"There is in the world a culture," he concludes. "It belongs to you, to me, to everybody. Computing is becoming a part of that.

"And, you see, if we are friends, if we are discussing something even with opposite points of view, then maybe we too can find a new brilliant idea."

Appendix 4: Communism in a High-tech Era: A Soviet View

The following excerpts are from an article in the Soviet journal *Voprosy Filosofii (Philosophical Questions)* 9, 1984, discussing the impact of new technologies on Marxist thought. The authors, N.N. Moiseev and I.T. Frolov, are corresponding members of the USSR Academy of Sciences. Entitled "A High Level of Interfacing: Society, Man, and Nature in the Age of Microelectronics, Information Science, and Biotechnology," the translated article appeared in the fall 1985 issue of *The Soviet Review* and is reprinted with the permission of M.E. Sharpe, Inc., Armonk, New York 10504.

A "high level of interfacing" is evidently the most appropriate term to apply when scientists and philosophers try to understand the present stage of the scientific and technological revolution and its perspectives relative to the development of microelectronics and bio-technology, to human society's entry into the age of robots and information science. Yet, it must be remembered that the new, higher level of technology of production must be accompanied by a new, higher level of development of society and of man himself in their interaction with nature. This presupposes in-depth social and philosophical research on the problems that arise here from the standpoint of Marxism, which, unfortunately, is still not a common feature in our or foreign literature. To be sure, there are already a number of fundamentally important works that constitute the basis of the Marxist tradition of analyzing these problems. Since we have, especially in recent years, had occasion to study these problems, albeit from different but nonetheless complementary aspects, and even to participate jointly in discussion of them, especially at international forums, we decided to try to present our ideas on a number of new questions, if only by way of formulating the problem and, in some cases, by way of discussion, without worrying about what are called the authorities, but also without ignoring what others have done. However, let us first say a few words about the scientific and technological aspect of the problems under discussion, without claiming that our exposition is systematic and complete, since this aspect has been quite well described in the specialized literature. . . .

The meaning of the information revolution is still not truly understood. We are only now beginning to understand its potential and consequences. At any rate, not until the eighties did it become clear, first, that this revolution was associated not only with the invention of the computer but also with the entire complex of electronic equipment, including communication lines, data display equipment, various kinds of reproduction equipment, etc. Second, it also became clear that it was impossible to solve the major scientific and technological problems of modern times without sophisticated data-processing and -analyzing systems, that modern data-processing and -analyzing systems, in combination with developed mathematical methods, make it possible to place on the agenda scientific problems that until recently seemed beyond the grasp of man. These problems include, in particular, the problem of creating an "artificial intelligence," the global study of processes in the biosphere, etc. And, finally, it is specifically the new means of transmitting and analyzing information that may prove to be the key to the implementation of programs for restructuring man's scale of values, which we shall discuss below.

In the history of the information revolution, no matter how brief it may have been, it is also possible to name several epochal events. The first of these is the invention of the computer, which occurred almost simultaneously and independently in the USA and the USSR in the late forties. For almost twenty years, computers were regarded primarily as superfast adding machines. The advent of the computer was truly an event whose significance is difficult to exaggerate. Without computers, space exploration, modern nuclear reactors, and many of the advances in physics and chemistry that we have witnessed would have been impossible. Since the late fifties, computers have been widely used in the economy, and this fact has had a significant influence on the whole nature of economic development.

The second epochal event was the advent of third-generation computers in the late sixties. This was probably the time of major breakthroughs in the history of computers. What happened then, and why can the entire history of the first two generations of computers be regarded merely as a kind of prehistory of the information revolution? From an engineering viewpoint, there was only a certain amount of improvement in the technology-integrated circuits and displays came into being, i.e., it became possible to display information on a television screen, and all elements were miniaturized, thus dramatically reducing the cost of arithmetic units; magnetic disks were developed that made it possible not only to expand the memory infinitely but also to greatly simplify access to stored information. And, finally, it was no less important that the inputting and outputting of information were also simplified. Although none of these innovations had a decisive influence on the fate of the computer, in their aggregate they qualitatively altered the role of the computer and its significance in science and society. It may even be that the computational aspect of computers has become a secondary factor in their use.

Third-generation computers have offered the possibility of a "man-computer" dialogue. And this is the key to combining formal and informal modes of reasoning. The computer can follow all manner of logical chains much more rapidly and precisely than man. Man, on the other hand, has a creative potential that is, to a considerable extent, fettered by the need to analyze numerous complex relationships. The possibility of simulating reality on a computer and of analyzing variants in a short period of time is specifically the level that is offered by the synthesis of the creative potential of man and the computer that realizes logical procedures. Notwithstanding the fact that a relatively short time has elapsed since the appearance of third-generation computers, the new technology for utilizing information has already had an appreciable impact on the nature of scientific research activity and on the improvement of management procedures in the national economy and in many other spheres of human activity.

The advent of personal computers (PCs) and telecommunications [*telematika*] was the third event of epochal significance in the early eighties. The development of compact, highly productive computers was a natural stage in the miniaturization of computing and memory devices; it was responsive to the logic of development of computer technology. The development of production technology led to a sharp reduction in cost: today even the most sophisticated PC costs no more than a medium-priced car. It remains to be added that an ordinary telephone is all that is needed to connect a PC to any mainframe computer so that the PC can be used as a terminal of the former.

The advent of inexpensive, compact, quite powerful, desk-size computers (as a rule, their capacity is no less than that of the renowned BESM-6), only slightly larger than an ordinary typewriter, has had, and will have, far-reaching consequences. The PC helps to intensify the labor of the scientist and designer and to alter the entire character of their work. The PC is so simple to operate that the assistance of a programmer is virtually unnecessary.

Small computers have an enormous impact on production activity. They are the key to robotization, to the transition from robot-manipulators to robots with self-contained computers. The availability of all features of third-generation computers, including display systems (the simplicity of operation plus extremely low cost), makes it possible to use them in management systems at any level and to analyze variants effectively. All these factors make PCs a new means of intensifying scientific and technical progress.

But everything that has been said above is still not the most important consideration. The reason why a PC is called a personal computer is that it is becoming a part of everyday life, just like the washing machine and the automobile. . . . It may be that the direct economic effect of the fact that a PC owner can use it to pay bills and keep a household budget is not so great. But the fact that computerization is becoming an everyday phenomenon, that man from childhood on becomes accustomed to regarding the computer as an integral part of his life, is of great importance for the forming of modern man. A child playing one of the innumerable personal computer games sometimes masters programming skills before he is fully able to read and write (interestingly, the art of programming is learned most readily in childhood). Can it be that computer languages are easier than traditional languages?

The word *telecommunications* is sometimes used in connection with the acronym *PC*. This term is used with increasing frequency to denote the linkage of computers, television, and various means of data transmission, including communication satellites. The principal task (or one of the principal tasks) of telecommunications is mass dissemination of information and making knowledge simultaneously accessible in all corners of the world. One example of the potential of telecommunications is telebridges such as the one of 1 November 1983 devoted to the consequences of a possible nuclear war. A

Soviet-American discussion devoted to this most important problem of modern times was held in two large rooms—one in Washington and one in Moscow —with large-screen television and simultaneous interpreting facilities. Each speaker was able to see two audiences simultaneously—Soviet and American—before him. He was in direct communication with his listeners. He could see their reaction and answer questions posed by listeners in both audiences.

Such telebridges, telelectures, and exchanges of information among people located in different continents are a powerful means of bridging the information and technology gap and developing a common view on one or another subject. Such means for influencing great masses of people have an enormous potential. It is difficult to imagine the formation of future man without the use of telecommunications. And in precisely the same way, development of the compromises that are so necessary in an age in which ecological problems become a dominant factor in our life on earth will require equally broad discussion. But like any technical innovation, telecommunications entails not only new potentialities but new dangers as well. Although it possesses enormous creative informational force, it can also act as a destabilizing factor: it all depends on who controls telecommunications. The various forms of use of microelectronics and telecommunications become particularly dangerous when these means fall into the hands of the military-industrial complex. Their ever-greater use in nuclear missile technology in the service of imperialism's aggressive goals increases the danger to human civilization. Only humane use of microelectronics and telecommunications can promote the development of civilization.

Thus, we see that the development of microelectronics has logically led to a new stage in the scientific and technological revolution at a time when human civilization has entered an age of robots and information science that transform the production sphere and the entire life of modern man. . . .

Socialist society fully evaluates the revolutionary potential and social consequences of microelectronics, information science, and biotechnology. It opens up broad opportunities for such applications and, at the same time, in its very essence corresponds most fully to this new technology, which requires that vast social capital rather than private capital—even if it may exceed the material resources of socialism for a certain period of time—be brought into play (on a planned basis). The socialist social structure makes it possible to use the basic potential of new technology—its labor-saving character—to the fullest. What is more, this does not entail the increase in unemployment that is inevitable under capitalism.

This is the major advantage of socialism and the fundamental basis for the "high degree of its interfacing" with new technology. On this basis, socialist countries have, in recent years, made vigorous efforts to intensify social production through the incorporation of advances in scientific-technical progress in social production, *inter alia,* for the most part, in microelectronics, information science, and biotechnology. Decisions of the Twenty-sixth CPSU Congress and subsequent decrees of the CPSU Central Committee and the Soviet government that related particularly to the development of microprocessor technology, to robot production, and to promoting the progress of biotechnology have provided a powerful impetus to the progress of the scientific and technological revolutions in the new stage. . . .

Notes

1. Frederick R. Starr, "Technology and Freedom in the Soviet Union," *Technology Review* (May-June 1984): 42.

2. "World Market Fueled by New Technology," *1987 World Outlook* (January 1987): 1. (Published in the United Kingdom by Telecommunications Industry Research).

3. For the evolution of Soviet ideological attitudes on postindustrial society, see Robbin Laird, "Post-industrial Society: East and West," *Survey* (London) 21 (Autumn 1975): 1-17. Ambivalent official Soviet attitudes about the role of information in a postindustrial environment are discussed in Nicholas Ulanov, "Soviet Fear of the Knowledge Revolution," *Wall Street Journal,* 13 May 1986, 19.

4. Alex Beam, "We Should Elevate Computerization to Superproject Status," *Business Week,* 11 November 1985, 102. (Included in "Russia Gropes for a Way to Enter the High-tech Age," 98-102.)

5. I.T. Frolov and N.M. Moiseev, "A High Level of Interfacing: Society, Man and Nature in the Age of Microelectronics, Information Science and Biotechnology," *Voprosy Filosofii* 9 (1984). (Reprinted in English translation in *The Soviet Review* 26, 3 (Fall 1985): 42-70.

6. Quoted in Paul Walton and Paul Tate, "Soviets Aim for Fifth Gen," *Datamation,* 1 July 1984, 56.

7. Marshall I. Goldman, "Gorbachev's Risk in Reforming the Soviet Economy," *Technology Review,* April 1986, 19.

8. "Gorbachev Policy Gains as Three Allies Advance in Party," *New York Times,* 27 June 1987, 5.

9. "On the Party's Tasks in Radically Restructuring the Management of the Economy, Report by M.S. Gorbachev, General Secretary of the CPSU Central Committee, at the Central Committee Plenum 25 June 1987," *Pravda,* 26 June 1987, 1-5. English translation by Foreign Broadcast Information Service FBIS-SOV-123, 26 June 1987, R-25.

10. Joseph Berliner, *The Innovation Decision in Soviet Industry* (Cambridge, Mass.: MIT Press, 1976), 8-18.

11. Marshall I. Goldman, "Gorbachev and Economic Reform," *Foreign Affairs* (Fall 1985): 67.

12. Ivan Selin, "Communications and Computers in Soviet Union," *Signal* 40,4 (December 1986): 93.

13. "At Soviet Writers Meeting, Jeers amid a New Daring," *New York Times,* 30 June 1986, 6.

14. *Nauka i Zhizn* 10 (1985): 22.

15. A.P. Ershov, *"EVM v Shkole," Pravda,* 8 February 1985. Quoted in "Soviet Leaders Grapple with the Scientific and Technological Revolution," *Radio Liberty Research Report,* RL 192-85, 14 June 1985, 4.

16. E.F. Melnik, *"ASU v Pravovom Aspekte," Sovetskoe Gosudarstvo i Pravo* 1 (1985): 126. Quoted in *Radio Liberty Research Report,* RL 192-85, 14 June 1985, 5.

17. Zbigniew Brzezinski, *Between Two Ages* (New York: Viking Press, 1970), 146.

18. "On Measures to Strengthen the Material and Technical Base and to Develop Telephone Communications Services Provided for the Population in 1986–90 and the Period through the Year 2000." Resolution of the Central Committee of the Communist Party of the Soviet Union and the USSR Council of Ministers, adopted 23 January 1985, *Pravda,* 26 February 1985, 1. Translation in "USSR National Affairs: Economic Development," Foreign Broadcast Information Service, 1 March 1985, S-1.

19. "Eleventh Five-Year Plan Successfully Completed: Report of the USSR Central Statistical Board," *Pravda,* 26 January 1986, 1. Translated in *Reprints from the Soviet Press,* 42, 5, 15 March 1986, 44.

20. Talk by A.A. Aleshin, head of the USSR Ministry of Communications main administration of urban and rural communications. Moscow domestic radio service in Russian, 17 March 1985. Translated in Joint Publications Research Services JPRS-TTP-85-010, 16 April 1985, 33-35.

21. "Makes Means of Communication Reliable and Efficient," *Pravda,* 26 September 1985, 1. Translated in *The Current Digest of the Soviet Press* 37, 39 (1985): 23.

22. Gayle Durham Hannah, *Soviet Information Networks* (Washington, D.C.: Center for Strategic and International Studies, 1977), 23.

23. David K. Willis, *Klass: How Russians Really Live* (New York: St. Martin's Press, 1985), 152.

24. Resolution of the CPSU Central Committee and the USSR Council of Ministers, adopted 23 January 1985, *Pravda,* 26 February 1985, 1. Translation by FBIS, "USSR National Affairs," 1 March 1985, S-1.

25. Aleshin, Moscow domestic radio service, 17 March 1985. Translated in JPRS-TTP-85-010, 16 April 1985, 34.

26. Moscow domestic radio in Russian, 18 June 1985. Reported in *Survey of Soviet Media,* British Broadcasting Corporation BBC SU-W1346-B-2, 5 July 1985.

27. Harriet R. Shinn and S. Blake Swensrud, "Intersputnik: Current Status and Future Options" (Working Paper for International Communications Program, Center for Strategic and International Studies, September 1984), 4.

28. "Disconnected," *The Economist* (London), 3 July 1982, 37.

29. William K. McHenry, "The Absorption of Computerized Management Information Systems in Soviet Enterprise" (Ph.D. diss., University of Arizona, 1985), 313.

30. R.J. Raggett, "Soviet C³I and the Question of Technology Transfer," *Signal* (December 1985): 18.

31. *"Glavcosmos* Formed by Soviets to Help Run Space Program," *Aviation Week and Space Technology,* 24 March 1986, 82. For a useful survey of Soviet satellite patterns, see Robert Campbell, "Satellite Communication in the USSR," *Soviet Economy* 1,4 (October-November 1985): 322-344.

32. For a survey of early Soviet computer developments, see N.C. Davis and S.E. Goodman, "The Soviet Bloc's Unified System of Computers," *Computing Surveys* 10, 2 (June 1978): 94-100.

33. Soviet acquisition priorities are identified in *Soviet Acquisition of Militarily Significant Western Technology: An Update* (U.S. Department of Defense white paper, September 1985), 1.

34. Paul Tate and David Hebditch, "Opening Moves," *Datamation,* 15 March 1987, 45. (See appendix 3 for full text of article).

35. McHenry, "Absorption of Computerized Management Information Systems," 265.

36. *Soviet Acquisition of Militarily Significant Western Technology,* 7.

37. Aleksandrov's comments were reported in an interview carried by *Izvestia,* 10 June 1985.

38. B. Naumov, *"Personal'nye EVM na Starte," Izvestia,* 11 July 1986. See Philip Hanson, *Radio Free Europe,* "A Slow Start for Personal Computers in the USSR," *Radio Liberty Research Report* RL 352-86, 15 September 1986, 1.

39. Ross Stapleton and Seymour Goodman, "Microcomputing in the Soviet Union and Eastern Europe," *Abacus* 3, 1 (Fall 1985): 6-22.

40. Hanson, "A Slow Start," RL 352-86, 1.

41. Tate and Hebditch, "Opening Moves," 43.

42. Ross Stapleton, "Soviet and East European Microcomputer Systems," *Signal* (December 1985): 69-76.

43. Tate and Hebdicht, "Opening Moves," 43.

44. McHenry, "Absorption of Computerized Management Information Systems," 32.

45. For a detailed description of Soviet data-bank administration, see "USSR State Information Systems and Resources," *Transnational Data and Communication Report* (August 1986): 22-24.

46. " *'Ornament': Bank initsiativi," Izvestia,* 13 March 1987. See "Private Data Banks in the Soviet Union?", *Radio Free Europe,* 24 April 1987, 1-3.

47. "Soviets Plugged into Western Computer Networks," *Transnational Data and Communication Report* (March 1987): 5-7.

48. "East Europe Data Services Assessed," *Transnational Data and Communication Report* (March 1987): 9-10.

49. "Vienna Group, Child of Détente, Tightens its Belt," *New York Times,* 18 January 1984, 13.

50. Jorg Becker, "West-East Data Transfer: the German Connection," *Transnational Data and Communication Report* (August 1986): 11-14.

51. Interview with Andrei Ershov, "We Should Elevate Computerization to Superproject Status," *Business Week,* 11 November 1985, 102.

52. Viktor Washmann, "Personal Computers in the Soviet Union: Technology and Politics," *Radio Liberty Research Report,* RL 308-84, 14 August 1984, 5.

53. Martin Cave, "Computers and the Organization of Information in the USSR" (Paper presented at the Third World Congress for

Soviet and East European Studies, Washington, D.C., October 1985), 14.

54. Jiri Pehe, "The New, and Democratizing, Soviet Middle Class," *New York Times,* 25 May 1987, 19.

55. This prospect was advanced by Secretary of State George P. Shultz in a speech to the Stanford Alumni Association in March 1986. See "Shultz Says Technology May Aid in Easing East-West Tensions," *New York Times,* 21 March 1986, 1.

56. Quoted in *Time,* 15 April 1985, 84.